# UP AND DOWN IN ADRIA

# UP AND DOWN
# IN ADRIA

SOME CONSIDERATIONS OF THE
VOLUME ENTITLED *SOUNDINGS*

BY

## E. L. MASCALL

'Where lies the land to which the ship would go?
Far, far ahead, is all her seamen know.'
A. H. CLOUGH

## THE FAITH PRESS
7 TUFTON STREET LONDON SW 1

FIRST PUBLISHED, 1963

© E. L. Mascall, 1963

PRINTED IN GREAT BRITAIN
in 10pt TIMES ROMAN TYPE
BY THE FAITH PRESS LTD
LEIGHTON BUZZARD

# STELLAE MARIS

# CONTENTS

Acknowledgment is due to the Syndics of the Cambridge University Press for permission to quote from the volume *Soundings: Essays concerning Christian Understanding*, edited by Dr. A. R. Vidler and published by them.

# INTRODUCTION
## NO BOTTOM YET

I HAVE written this little book with feelings of both reluctance and trepidation. For one single theologian, who has received no special commission for the task, to take it upon himself to criticize the writings of ten of his colleagues who must be assumed to be experts in the particular subjects on which they have chosen to write might indeed savour of foolhardiness no less than of presumption. Furthermore, all of the writers in question are men for whom I have considerable respect, most of them are acquaintances and not a few are personal friends. Nevertheless, like the Victorian poet, I do but sing because I must, though, also like him, I am conscious of the uncomplimentary interpretations that may be put upon my piping. And my feeling that some really searching examination of the symposium *Soundings* is called for, both in its general approach and in the details of its execution, is fortified by the Editor's explicit statement in his Introduction that he and his crew—for that term, rather than 'team,' would seem to be appropriate in view of the title that they have chosen for their work—so far from wishing to evade the assessment of their work by their contemporaries, will in fact welcome it.

Now any general and overall judgment which may be passed on a collection of eleven essays by ten different writers must obviously be subject to a great many individual exceptions, especially when, as the Editor explains is true in the present case, the writers' desire is to stimulate thought rather than to enforce a party line or a rule of orthodoxy. And it will, I hope, be clear from my subsequent discussion that there is in *Soundings* a great deal with which I thoroughly agree, much from which I am grateful to have learnt, and not a little speculation which seems to me to be both legitimate and stimulating. It must also be recognized that contributors to a symposium have a tendency to go their own way and that their discussions are not always recognizable as examples of the outlook described in the editorial preface. In the present case this is, I think, specially true of the two essays by Mr. Woods and largely true about those by Professor Smart and Professor Burnaby. Nevertheless, the book as a whole is permeated by a certain general attitude which is accurately described by the Editor and it is one which in my view is both regrettable and unnecessary.

'We believe,' the Editor writes, 'that there are very important questions which theologians are now being called upon to face, and which are not yet being faced with the necessary seriousness and determination. We do not profess yet to see our way through them: and we do not want to have to reproach ourselves with looking for a way round them. Our task is to see what the questions are that we ought to be facing in the nineteen-sixties.' With this I entirely agree, but I am not at all happy about the questions which they select for discussion or the criteria to which they look in their attempt to move towards a solution. Those which they have chosen are indeed of great importance, and one cannot quarrel with their decision not to try to cover the whole theological field but to restrict themselves to their own special interests. Nevertheless, one might expect them to show more awareness than they do of the very wide range of questions that are under active discussion outside their own somewhat restricted and specialized circle, especially as some of these have considerable bearing upon the problems with which they themselves are concerned.

One cannot but admire the modesty with which Dr. Vidler's Leadsmen (for that would seem to be the right term by which to describe them) view their own achievements. 'We believe,' he writes, 'we are handling questions that are not likely to receive definitive answers for a long time to come.' And in view of the notorious tendency of scholars in the past to claim virtual finality for their conclusions in such fields as the historical and literary investigations of Christian origins, such reluctance to commit themselves is, in its place, admirable. But what is its place? It is, I would suggest, those realms of study in which the scholar has nothing to rely upon except the intellectual competence of himself and his colleagues. It is, however, much less satisfactory when what is at stake is nothing less than the basic affirmations of Christian faith and morals, the tradition, the *paradosis*, the whole *via vitae* of the Christian Church. I think a great many readers will feel shocked and scandalized when they see how little guidance a group of avowed Christians, all but one of whom are Anglican priests who either have or have recently had pastoral responsibilities, have to offer to their contemporaries in the doctrinal and moral chaos of the present day. 'We do not all point in the same direction . . .,' writes the Editor. 'We are thankful all to be in the same ship; whatever we do not know, we know that the ship is afloat; and the fact that we make these soundings is evidence of our conviction that there is a bottom to the sea.' What is the ground of this conviction we are not told, and in any case the Leadsmen make no claim to have found bottom. Now we may, I think, agree with the Editor when he claims that 'it is not only obtuseness or incompetence that prevents us from adumbrating a re-interpretation of the Christian faith comparable with that so courageously and confidently essayed by the authors of *Lux Mundi*.' The present situation may well be one in which it would be wiser to attend to the exposition of the Christian faith in modern terms rather than to its re-interpretation. Many of the Leadsmen, however, seem to have lost all confidence in the tradition that they have received and to envisage their task simply as, in Mr. Root's phrase, 'beginning all over again,' as if we had nothing to learn from nineteen centuries of Christian experience; thus, for example Mr. Williams calls for a complete reconstruction of Christian morals on the basis of one not universally accepted contemporary psychological theory, and Mr. Montefiore attempts a similar reconstruction of Christology on the basis of a meta-physical outlook which is already obsolescent. It will, I think, be found that Christianity has been intellectually most vigorous and influential when it has been clearest about its own inheritance and at the same time most aware of the needs and deficiencies of the contemporary world. The Leadsmen, however, seem for the most part to be more confident in the contemporary world's estimate of the realities of the human situation than they are in the great tradition of thought and life that they have inherited as members of the Church. In making this criticism, I do not wish in the least to imply that the tradition is a rigid and finished product that can be applied to the contemporary situation like an antiseptic plaster or that it is not subject from time to time to distortions and divagations. On the contrary, it is a living and growing reality whose content and possibilities we have hardly begun to discover. It may at the present time have largely lost touch with the world that surrounds it, or, perhaps we may prefer to say, the world has largely lost touch with it. But in itself, I am convinced, it holds all the resources that we need for this as for any other age, and the urgent task for the theologian today is first that he should live within it and do all that is in his power to penetrate into its riches, secondly that he should play whatever part he is able to play in developing its latent possibilities, and thirdly that he should, in his aspect of apologist and evangelist, do all that he can to integrate the life and thought of the contemporary world into it. And this will involve us in intellectual activity every bit as exacting and, for all we know, in conclusions every bit as exciting as any that Dr. Vidler and his Leadsmen have engaged in. My first criticism of *Soundings,* then, is that, taking it in its overall character, it has misunderstood the function of the Christian theologian *vis-à-vis* the contemporary world. My second criticism is that it has ignored a lot of contemporary questions which it ought to have faced.

Dr. Vidler may appear to have disarmed this second criticism by his reminder that the Leadsmen were a limited group and that there are plenty of other subjects that might have been included and that another group of essayists might have taken up. It must be replied that some of these other questions are extremely fundamental and that many of the topics that *are* discussed in *Soundings* cannot be satisfactorily discussed unless these more basic questions have received at least a provisional answer. This neglect is less excusable because a great deal of attention has in fact been given to some of these in ecumenical theological circles. There is, for example, the whole matter of the nature of grace and its relation to nature, which has received such a penetrating analysis in the little book which recently emerged from the conference at Chevetogne between a group of Roman Catholics, Orthodox and Calvinists. There is the question of the unity and authority of the Bible, which needs a far more profound solution than it receives anywhere in *Soundings*. There is the problem of the relation between Scripture and Tradition, which has been so strikingly reopened by Fr. Tavard in his book *Holy Writ or Holy Church,* and is at present exercising not only many Catholic and Protestant scholars on the Continent but also the highest authorities in the Roman Church. There is the question of doctrinal development, with all the implications which it has for the reunion of Christendom; Dr. Owen Chadwick, in his book *From Bossuet to Newman,* has provided a superb historical survey of the material but no Anglican theologian seems to have thought the problem itself worthy of his attention. There is the problem of the nature of the Church and of the Sacraments, on which again most fruitful interchanges have taken place in the ecumenical field. There is the problem of sacrifice, which stretches all the way from primitive religion to the Christian Eucharist, and on which the researches of anthropologists no less than the discussions of theologians have done much to overcome the antagonisms of four centuries of Christian disunity in the West. And behind all these there are the absolutely funda-

13

mental questions of the Being of the Triune God and of the relation of God to his creation, questions which have engaged the closest attention of thinkers such as St. Augustine, St. Thomas and St. Gregory Palamas in the past and have come to life again to-day. Now I suppose the Leadsmen might reply that all these are remote and technical subtleties, while they themselves are concerned with the commendation of the Christian faith to the contemporary man. However, if there is one thing that emerges from a reading of *Soundings* it is that the essayists are very far from clear in their own minds, and certainly very far from agreement with one another, about the nature of the Christian faith itself. This is, I suggest, mainly due to their almost complete avoidance of properly theological issues. They admit that their leads have not found bottom; perhaps the reason is that their soundings have not gone deep enough. This is, of course, a common failing of Anglican academic theologians. If one compares the present century with the last, it is almost frightening to observe how few Anglican holders of theological posts are concerned with strictly theological issues as distinct from matters of historical and literary criticism; and it is notorious how badly Anglicans show up at ecumenical gatherings in this respect.

I would repeat that I have written this account of *Soundings* in no spirit of hostility, though I have written it with a good deal of distress, distress which has been increased by a tendency in some quarters to acclaim the book as a profound and courageous statement of the word of the Church to this generation. I have nothing but admiration for the intention of the writers and, as will appear from my subsequent discussion, many of the things which they have said seem to me to be both true and important. But, taking it by and large, the book suffers, in my judgment, from three serious deficiencies. First, it fails to ask the really fundamental questions. Secondly, it looks to the wrong quarters for its answers. Thirdly, it fails to look to the quarters in which the answers might be, and to a large extent are already being, found.

I have accepted the open invitation of the Leadsmen to criticize their work, so I cannot be accused of gate-crashing. It is, nevertheless, polite to say Thank you for an invitation and I will do this in the words of St. Thomas. 'We must love them both,' the Angelic Doctor writes, 'those whose opinions we share and those whose opinions we reject. For both have laboured in the search for truth and both have helped us in the finding of it.' [1]

[1] *In Met.*, 12, 9.

# CHAPTER I

## SETTING THE COURSE

I PROPOSE to consider together in this chapter the first three essays in the volume *Soundings,* as they are all, in one way or another, concerned with what man can know about God, at least in principle, without the direct aid of the Christian revelation. Mr. H. E. Root writes about the present predicament of natural theology, Dr. J. S. Habgood about the relations between science and theology, and Mr. G. F. Woods about the particular problems raised by the divine transcendence.

Mr. Root gives to his essay the title 'Beginning all over again,' and this is in itself characteristic of an assumption which is common to most, though not, I think, all of the Leadsmen, that there is really very little help for present-day theologians to be gained from the nineteen centuries of Christian thought that have preceded them. It will, I hope, appear from my subsequent discussion that the great tradition of Christendom has more resources than they suppose, and I cannot help thinking that, both in solving their own problems and in giving to others the guidance that they are anxious to give, they would have done well to take it more seriously than they do. Be that as it may, it is clearly Mr. Root's avowed intention to take us back to port and, with his lead in his hand, to set out upon a more satisfactory course than Christians have sailed on in the past.

Mr. Root begins by making it plain what he means by natural theology. Taking his definition from the *Oxford Dictionary of the Christian Church* he tells us that it is 'that body of knowledge [about God] which may be obtained by human reason alone without the aid of revelation' (I take it that the words which I have enclosed within brackets were omitted by him by accident and not by design). It is, he tells us, generally agreed that natural theology so defined is in a poor state and

16

not every one agrees that this is unfortunate. 'Natural theology, outside Catholic traditions, has generally been regarded as the poor relation if not the black sheep of the family. Theologians have never been convinced that he had a proper job of work to do.' I presume that in this last sentence we are to take 'never' as meaning 'not always' or else 'convinced' as meaning 'agreed,' for I cannot suppose that Mr. Root really means to exclude St. Thomas Aquinas, Butler, A. E. Taylor, Dr. A. M. Farrer or his fellow-Leadsman Mr. G. F. Woods from the ranks of the theologians. 'On the other side,' he goes on, 'philosophers have seldom been happy to acknowledge the philosophical theologian as one of their family.' This is perhaps less disputable, though even here 'very often not' might be more accurate than 'seldom.' It is, however, undoubtedly true that there are large groups of both theologians and philosophers to-day who reject the whole notion of natural theology, either because they hold that we can only know God by revelation or that we cannot give an intelligible content to the notion of God at all. However, no doubt with his pastoral responsibility as a Christian priest in mind, Mr. Root makes it plain that he is not very much concerned with the special problems of either theologians or philosophers but with the general mass of men and women to-day. Thus he writes in a striking passage:

> It would be wildly disproportionate to claim that the rescue of natural theology was in itself the most important task confronting Christianity and the Church in the twentieth century. It would be almost as wild to claim that recent philosophical criticism of traditional arguments in natural theology was in our time the only formidable intellectual challenge to faith. The great problem of the Church (and therefore of its theologians) is to establish or re-establish some kind of vital contact with that enormous majority of human beings for whom Christian faith is not so much unlikely as irrelevant and uninteresting. The greatest intellectual challenge to faith is simply that thoroughly secularized intelligence which is now the rule rather than the exception, whether it expresses itself in science or philosophy or politics or the arts.

Here I thoroughly agree, with a mild cavil about the inclusion of 'science' in the last sentence; I should not have thought that, so long as it kept to its own job, science as such could express itself as either for or against religion. (There are of course important questions about the relations of science and religion which scientists can usefully discuss if they are competent in both fields, but they are not questions for science as such.) When Mr. Root goes on to write that 'if the health of natural theology matters, it matters only because it is bound up with more important things,' I think he is quite right, but it needs to be added that this is true not only of natural theology. It is equally true of electrical engineering, stockbroking, politics, portrait painting, music and Biblical exegesis, in fact of all human pursuits. All these are, from the Christian point of view, only of any *ultimate* value if, whether proximately or remotely, they assist men and women to attain the vision of God and the resurrection from the dead as members of Christ's Body. But this does not prevent them from having a relative but none the less authentic value of their own, so long as the ends to which they are directed are not sinful, because they are in fact expressions of the nature and endowments of man as God has made him. And I would suggest that their practitioners will in fact realize their several vocations more perfectly if they are not *always* consciously thinking about man's last end and if, while they are actually engaged in their task, they simply concentrate upon doing it as well as possible. And just as a surgeon who is a Christian when he is performing a delicate and difficult operation, will serve God best by concentrating all his attention upon the job in hand, so the natural theologian, when he is doing his natural theology, will serve God best by doing the best natural theology of which he is capable rather than by concerning himself at that moment with its power to interest and attract those who are outside the Church. This does not mean that at other times he may not consider the relevance of his special work to the latter task. But when he is doing that he will be doing apologetics and not natural theology, and one impression that I derive from Mr. Root's essay is that he is not altogether clear about the difference between the two. I would therefore urge that, at the present day, the primary task of the natural theologian is to take note of the objections that have been urged against the possibility of natural theology by some schools of theologians and by some schools of philosophers and to reconstruct his natural theology in such a way that it will be impervious to these attacks. He will, in this way, be performing a task that will indirectly be of great benefit to apologetics, just as the bacteriologist will be performing a task that is of great benefit to social welfare; but, just as the bacteriologist when he is in his laboratory should be concerned not with social welfare but with bacteria, so the natural theologian when he is in his study should be concerned not with apologetics but with natural theology.

It is, I think, partly at least, through failing to make this necessary distinction that Mr. Root is so ready to scrap all the natural theology of the past and, to use his own phrase 'begin all over again.' And he seems to show a peculiar lack of attention to some of the work that has been done on natural theology in recent years by writers who have certainly not been unaware of the contemporary assaults on their subject. Thus, for example, he makes no mention of Dr. A. M. Farrer's great, and by no means unoriginal, work *Finite and Infinite*, of the collective work *Faith and Logic*, or of his fellow-Leadsman Mr. Woods's book *Theological Explanation*, and his only reference to the symposium *Prospect for Metaphysics* is to a remark of Professor Ninian Smart's to the effect that natural theology is 'the sick man of Europe,' in spite of the fact that the concluding essay in that book, Professor H. D. Lewis's 'God and Mystery,' is one of the most brilliant and penetrating defences of natural theology that has been produced in recent years.[1] It is perhaps understandable, but in

---

[1] Professor Lewis's important book *Our Experience of God* no doubt appeared too late for Mr. Root to notice it.

my opinion no less regrettable, that he ignores also such remarkable works by Roman Catholic writers as those of Father Lonergan and Dom Illtyd Trethowan. It is in fact striking that, while he mentions what he describes as 'the useful but distracting work' exemplified by the volume entitled *New Essays in Philosophical Theology,* although he says that its 'novelty was not striking,' he makes no mention of the defences of natural theology that that volume contains, for he makes it plain that he thinks there is no future in that kind of approach. I agree with him that the darts of the sceptics are not to be turned aside by talk about revelation, Biblical categories, history and eschatology, but I see no valid reason for his rejection of the classical model of natural theology, though I would admit that it needs plenty of *aggiornamento.* He does not, let us be quite clear about this, reject natural theology as such, but he has already told us that 'a restoration of natural theology will finally depend upon the abandonment of our present understanding of what it is.' And so —'beginning all over again.'

'Christian theology without metaphysics (that is, for our purposes, natural theology) is an illusion.' Mr. Root repeats, 'However much some theologians may wish to avoid the issue by speaking of revelation there comes a point when the question can no longer be evaded: Why believe in God at all? . . . The special task of a Christian metaphysic, natural theology, is to show the grounds for that total picture of the world which we indicate when we speak of the Christian faith.' And this, he tells us, while it is a picture of the world in so far as it is articulated in theologies, doctrines and creeds, is more than a picture in that it commends and inculcates attitudes and feelings which are more than descriptive, namely religious practices, prayer and worship. Now according to Mr. Root, the trouble with the accepted model of natural theology is that, although the logical form of argument to which it is wedded was at one time surrounded with an atmosphere of imagination and excitement (he interestingly compares it with the excitement engendered earlier in this century by the logical discoveries of Russell and Whitehead), this is so no longer. Natural theology has thus fallen into debility and poverty because it has become divorced from the deepest sources of intellectual and artistic creativity. Now, the argument continues, 'where do we look now for faithful, stimulating, profound accounts of what it is to be alive in the twentieth century? . . . We look to the poet or novelist or dramatist or film producer.' And so 'the best text-books for contemporary natural theologians are not the second-hand theological treatises but the living works of artists who are in touch with the springs of creative imagination.'

This is indeed a formidable programme, but we ought not to be deterred by lack of courage. It does, however, raise a number of problems to which Mr. Root gives little or no attention. We may perhaps ignore the implied sneer at theological treatises as being 'second-hand,' but we must stress the fact that, with his repudiation of logic in favour of the art of the poet, novelist, dramatist or film producer, Mr. Root has deprived natural theology of the status of a rational pursuit altogether. It may, of course, be argued that art, in some of its modes and aspects, has a cognitive function—the late W. G. De Burgh argued this in his posthumously published work *The Life of Reason*—but unless we are to lapse into complete subjectivity we need the use of logic and reason to discriminate in art between the veridical and the purely fanciful. The poet, the novelist, the dramatist and the film producer may be depicting a world of pure dreams. There have indeed been, and there are to-day, Christian poets, novelists, dramatists, and possibly film producers too, who have brought to life, by their inspired use of imaginative media, the doctrines of the Christian faith in a way which may well lead the professional theologian to despair and, like the painter in *Kai Lung* who observed a damsel of surpassing beauty, to destroy the instruments of his craft and set up again in life as a trainer of performing elephants. I have in mind Dorothy

Sayers and Charles Williams, Mr. W. H. Auden's poem-cycle *For the Time Being* and Dr. C. S. Lewis's inter-planetary novels. But such writers are usually the first to recognize the importance of natural theology of the rational type and can be intensely interested and excited by it.[2] And without such rational support I do not see how the modern man is to decide between the various interpretations of the world and of human existence which different artists put before them. 'Theologians,' Mr. Root tells us, 'cannot direct men's minds to God until they are themselves steeped in God's world and in the imaginative productions of his most sensitive and articulate creatures.' I am not sure what are the criteria by which sensitivity and articulateness are to be judged, but I suspect that their application might well lead nineteenth-century people to take their interpretation of life from the *Rubaiyat* of Edward FitzGerald and twentieth-century people to take theirs from the films of Ingmar Bergman. Furthermore, it is a common complaint of artists themselves to-day, no less than of Christian theologians, that, in contrast with artists of previous ages, they find it for the most part extremely difficult to communicate with the contemporary world. And even when, as with some of Mr. Eliot's plays,

[2] Thus Charles Williams, reviewing a book on natural theology of a very traditional type wrote: 'There was a moment . . . when I found myself savouring a particular doctrine with an almost physical delight; and, except from false fear, I do not know why I say almost. It was in my mouth "sweet as honey"; it melted exquisitely into my corporal organism and bestowed a richness. Perhaps the Apocalyptic John was talking more sense than we know when he spoke of "eating a book." It would be humbling if we discovered that the saints and prophets were physiologically as well as psychologically accurate. . . . The particular doctrine in question was that of the self-sufficiency of God. . . . How burdensome the opposite view, that creation is necessary to God! heretical, though taken by distinguished minds. It is so often assumed that the great philosophical doctrines are inhuman, but it is not so; their high abstractions thunder in our blood and our virtues feed on them. The web of created glory, exterior to himself, is unnecessary to himself. So the Divine Word need not have had a Mother, but exquisitely decreed that he would. So we need not love, but mightily decide that we will' (*Time and Tide,* 9 October, 1943, p. 828).

22

some definite impact has been made, it has been upon a comparatively sophisticated few, and even then the religious truth
which the dramatist has tried so hard to convey through his
particular medium has often failed to strike to the heart of
those who were not already converted. I should myself find
Mr. Root's programme exciting if he had given us any clear
indication of what it involved and what principles of discrimination it proposed to apply. But in place of this he concludes his essay with a page of moving but uninformative
rhetoric. For decades, if not generations, he tells us, the
Christian faith has lived in a state of imaginative impoverish-
ment and the Church has lived in almost total isolation from
the arts; this is no doubt true. And the theologian is warned
not to seek security by turning himself into an historian or
bibliographer or textual critic; this is indeed a salutary moni-
tion, as may be seen if we reflect on the shocking neglect in
contemporary Anglicanism of dogmatic theology, ascetic theology, liturgical theology and Christian sociology, though I do
not think this was what Mr. Root had in mind. 'We shall have
to contemplate and absorb the disturbing visions of human
nature which find expression in serious modern literature.'
But may not the Christian pastor find his material nearer at
hand in the lives of the flesh-and-blood men and women
whom God has given him to tend? 'We shall have to come to
terms with a world in which old patterns of morality no
longer direct or inspire because they no longer have life.' I
am not quite sure what 'coming to terms' with the world
means, but it is at least arguable that the Church has come to
terms with the world a great deal too much in the course of
her history, and there is something in the New Testament
about not being conformed to the world but being transformed by the renewing of our minds. It was precisely because
it refused to abandon its own patterns of morality and come
to terms with the world of its day that the Christian Church
in the early centuries was able to bring about a moral regeneration of society. 'We shall have to admit that we have

no ready answers to the questions people ask because for so long we have insulated ourselves against their questions.' If this is so, it is a cause for shame, but I suspect that our failure has lain not in insulating ourselves against the questions, or in failing to contemplate and absorb the disturbing visions of modern literature, but in failing to contemplate and absorb the inspiring visions and profound truths of the Christian revelation, those truths which, in Charles Williams's words, can be savoured with an almost physical delight. 'Good things as well as bad,' writes Professor C. S. Lewis, 'are caught by a kind of infection. If you want joy, power, peace, eternal life, you must get close to, or even into, the thing that has them. . . . They are a great fountain of energy and beauty spurting up from the very centre of reality. If you are close to it, the spray will wet you: if you're not, you will remain dry. Once a man is united to God, how could he *not* live for ever. Once a man is separated from God, what *can* he do but wither and die.' [3] It is this conviction of the living and life-giving character of the divine realities which I find so depressingly absent from the attitude of Mr. Root and most of his fellow-Leadsmen, with their reluctance to contemplate and feed upon the eternal verities and to hand on the fruit of their contemplation to others (*contemplari et contemplata aliis tradere*), their loss of nerve and of faith, not only in themselves but in the glories that they have inherited, not only in the earthen vessels but in the treasure that is within them, so that they find themselves driven for inspiration to a pagan world. If we have no other answers to give than those which we can find in the artistic expressions of a secularized society, we would seem to be very much in the position of a medical man who expected his patients to provide him with the remedies for their ailments. 'The starting point for natural theology,' Mr. Root asserts, 'is not argument but sharpened awareness.' Indeed, but awareness of what? 'It will take decades or generations,' he tells us, 'before we know whether natural theology [and

[3] *Beyond Personality*, p. 27.

we have seen that for him natural theology is confused with apologetics and pastoral solicitude] still has enough life in it to seek new kinds of nourishment.' And during the decades and generations while we are trying to find our way, how are Christ's sheep to be fed? It seems to me that it is Mr. Root, and not the despised traditionalists, who is retiring into an ivory castle with his poems and novels and plays and films, while the hungry and destitute world outside, for which he rightly feels such compassion, is dying for the food which he is commissioned to give it. If the trumpet sound such an uncertain note as this, who will prepare himself for the battle? It is shamefully true that we Christians, and not least we Christian priests, have been imperceptive, complacent and torpid, that, in the phrase of M. Jacques Maritain, we have made the eternal verities into a pillow. With nineteen centuries of Christian thinking, praying, living and dying to instruct, fortify and inspire us, I cannot think that the remedy for our present distress is simply to be found in beginning all over again; rather it consists in bringing out from our treasury the dazzling riches that we have inherited and have so sadly failed to appreciate, the sheer weight of glory that has been too splendid for our clouded eyes. I once knew a very distinguished theologian whose devoted wife used frankly to admit that 'X [mentioning her husband's Christian name] could make anything dull.' This is no doubt only too true of many of us. "Tis we, 'tis our estrangèd faces, that miss the many-splendoured thing.' The fault is in us, not in the gift that we have received. But, to repeat, all this is a matter of apologetics, not of natural theology.

I can comment on the other two chapters in the opening triad quite briefly, for there is little in them that I feel inclined to criticize. Dr. J. S. Habgood wisely warns us not to be complacent about the present truce between science and theology, which he describes as 'uneasy.' He points out that scientists to-day attribute much less metaphysical substantiality than did their predecessors to the fundamental entities of physics and a much less ultimate epistemological status to their theories; it might be added that those who are concerned with the philosophical aspect of science (the average working physicist, chemist or biologist is not) are very far from agreed as to what that epistemological status is; Dr. Mary B. Hesse's *Science and the Human Imagination* is very illuminating on this matter. Again, Dr. Habgood remarks that theology ought never to be a competitor with science in the empirical realm, and comments on the unnecessary confusion that has been produced by the fact that words such as 'origin' and 'creation' have been used by scientists and theologians in different senses without this being recognized. What seems to him to be far more serious, because it is far more real to-day, than any clash between science and theology is what he describes as the 'breakdown in communication,' and he holds that this is something deeper than the general fragmentation of knowledge that has been caused in the modern world by extreme specialization. Again, he points to the way in which science seems to give a great many scientists the kind of emotional satisfaction that many Christians get from their religion. Here I think he is quite right, and I think it is particularly true about cosmologists and geneticists, who can easily feel that they are on the verge of uncovering the ultimate secrets of the universe and of life. But it should perhaps be remembered that artists are exposed to a similar danger; the concluding chapter of M. Gilson's fascinating and entertaining book *Choir of Muses* contains a very serious and searching account of the difficulty for the artist of becoming a saint on account of the unconditionally demanding and absorbing character of his chosen pursuit. Once again, Dr. Habgood points to the impression, widely given, that, compared with that of science, the vision of theology often seems narrow and less evocative in its images. True once more, but, as I have said in discussing Mr. Root's essay, the fault is in Christians and not in the Faith and, with all respect, I must say that the Leadsmen seem to me to be every bit as drab in their outlook as their fellow-Christians and fellow-theologians. Dr. Habgood interestingly suggests that the remarkable success of Père Teilhard de Chardin's strange book *The Phenomenon of Man* lies in the breadth of vision and evocative power of its symbolic equipment which characterize it in spite of its vulnerability when considered from the purely scientific point of view.[4]

When he states his own contribution to the resolution of the 'uneasy tension,' Dr. Habgood points out that one thing that theology can do for science is to keep it constantly aware that, in spite of the apparently pragmatic nature of much of its theorizing and practice, it is ultimately concerned with truth and value. And this, he holds, means the deposition of the mathematical ideal of science, which has been produced by the immense prestige of physics and the exaltation of physics as the *regina scientiarum,* and the recovery of the idea of a hierarchy of sciences, based not upon their internal logical structure but upon the immediacy of their relationship to facts in the basic scientific sense of that word. In this way, he suggests, the psychological hold of mathematical ideals of scientific explanation may be removed and a positive relationship with theology be on the way to recovery; and he takes biology as an interesting borderline case and sociology as one not so much on the border. He warns us, however, against a too facile assumption that in this way we can just 'overarch the whole structure with the notion of "ultimate explanation" which only theology can provide' and remarks that many scientists and philosophers are understandably suspicious of such a procedure. He writes as follows, with considerable discrimination:

> Both sides perhaps are right. Scientific explanations are complete in relation to what they set out to do. And theology, if it seeks to raise ultimate questions, must at least search for some kind of ultimate explanation. The danger lies in upsetting the balance between these; either in ignoring the real element of discontinuity between the different levels of knowledge; or in acquiescing in too facile and radical a distinction.

[4] Cf. the very penetrating remarks on Teilhard by Dr. W. H. Thorpe in *Biology and the Nature of Man,* p. 15f.

> My main theological criticism of Teilhard de Chardin is that he blurs the discontinuity; my uneasiness about the writings of many others on science and theology is that they seem to imagine prematurely that by stating a distinction they have solved all the problems.

These are indeed interesting and stimulating suggestions that Dr. Habgood makes, and I hope that he will follow them up in detail elsewhere, for their adequate development clearly needs far more space than could be found in one essay of a symposium. I think that perhaps he might have allowed a little more weight than he has to some (I mean *some*, and not all!) of the large number of recent discussions of the subject, especially those written not by theologians but by scientists. Dr. J. D. Lambert's *Science and Sanctity*, Dr. William G. Pollard's *Physicist and Christian* and (perhaps with some reservations) Dr. R. E. D. Clark's *The Universe; Plan or Accident?* all seem to me to be significant in this respect, though it is just possible that they were not available when Dr. Habgood's essay was written. I am very much less happy about some of the books on the subject that have been written by theologians. But I fully agree with Dr. Habgood's conclusion, which is very much in line with the contention which I urged in the preface of my Bampton Lectures *Christian Theology and Natural Science*.

> Theological answers [he says] must not be given to scientific questions. Yet there is not a totally unbridgeable gulf between the two disciplines; nor are scientists and theologians totally different kinds of people with no subject-matter or methods in common. We must keep the conversation going in the belief that in the long run those who care about science will make better theologians, and those who care about theology, better scientists.

But I think the words 'in the long run' need to be emphasized.

Mr. G. F. Woods's essay on 'The Idea of the Transcendent' can be referred to very briefly indeed, not because it is trivial—that is far from being the case—but because I have really no fault to find with it. He takes a very limited but very important theme, namely the possibility of our making any intelligible statements about the transcendent Reality, and handles it very skilfully. I only wish that his fellow-Leadsman Mr. Montefiore had taken it more seriously before substituting a discussion of God's action upon us for a discussion of God's being in himself. Mr. Woods cogently remarks that, if we simply define the transcendent as what lies outside the limits of all human experience, we are bound to say that no one can ever experience it. But that, he alleges, is not what 'the transcendent' means and he embarks upon an illuminating investigation of the nature of analogical explanation; much more on these lines will, of course, be found in his book *Theological Explanation*, which does not seem to have received the attention to which its merits entitle it. Analogies, he tells us, do in fact work, however mysterious and, to some people, unexpected this may be. And 'no theory can be adequate which concludes that what happens cannot take place.' After some very useful clarificatory remarks, he affirms that we do have the experience of the transcendent, in the sense of having experience of beings which are other than our own, but 'we must try to look for it in the right way.' 'These experiences are not of observable physical features of these beings nor of ghostly replicas behind them but quite simply of their sheer presence. If we admit this experience, we are admitting that somehow we are not confined to the limits of our private experience in the sense that we cannot transcend our own experience sufficiently to acknowledge that other people and things are in existence, as well as ourselves.' But, Mr. Woods adds, 'we experience their presence in a wide variety of analogous ways.' These positions are very much in line with what I have frequently urged, that sensible phenomena are not the *objectum quod* of perception, but the *objectum quo*, through which we apprehend the *objectum quod* which is the trans-phenomenal intelligible being.[5] But Mr. Woods correctly observes that to say this is very far from

[5] Cf. my *Words and Images*, p. 70f.

saying that we can experience God, who is transcendent in a far more radical sense. However, he goes on to argue, in our experience of beings which come into and pass out of existence, we have a sense of the unchanging beneath the changes which we see. 'In our experience of the changing, we have also a curious experience of the unchanging. I believe that we are gradually driven towards an awareness of some being, which is variously styled pure, absolute, or transcendent. The conclusion is being itself. It is difficult to say whether one experiences this pure being or whether more usually one experiences being transcended by it.' (This last sentence seems to me to be particularly penetrating.) And, in expressing, or trying to express, this experience we make use of whatever analogies we can, often using several which, if taken not as analogies but as univocal descriptions, would be mutually inconsistent. 'The analogies of transcendence are instances of analogical explanations of the being and activity of God which are useful but never final or perfect.'

This general approach which Mr. Woods takes runs very much in line with those of a good many writers in recent years, such as Dr. Farrer, Dom Illtyd Trethowan and Dom Mark Pontifex, Professor H. D. Lewis and myself, though differences of detail are of course to be found. Mr. Woods opened his chapter with an expression of opinion by Professor R. W. Hepburn that 'the language of "transcendence" may well collapse into meaninglessness in the last analysis.' His own conclusion is that such an analysis has not been made and that it is unlikely that it will or can be made. For all the modesty of its scope and its treatment, this essay of Mr. Woods's seems to me to be one of the most useful things in the book, for if the position which he attacks could be maintained it would be the end of theology in anything like the traditional sense. Perhaps some of his fellow-Leadsmen would not be very much worried by such a collapse. But at least his essay bears out the Editor's statement that not all the contributors point in the same direction.

## CHAPTER II

## PUMPING OUT THE BILGE

WE have seen that in his Introduction the Editor of *Soundings*, speaking on behalf of his fellow-Leadsmen, has disclaimed with almost excessive modesty any claim to have found bottom; the most that he is prepared to assert is that the ship is afloat and that there must be a bottom to the sea. In less metaphorical terms he describes their aims as that of raising certain very important theological questions that are not being faced as they should be. 'We do not,' he says, 'profess yet to see our way through them.' [1] However, in Mr. H. A. Williams's essay, which bears the title 'Theology and Self-awareness,' a much more far-reaching claim seems to be made, for we are asked to adopt in the realm of ethics an altogether new approach which by-passes the whole ethical tradition of Christendom and to accept certain conclusions about Christian behaviour which are at variance with the accepted moral teaching of Christianity. Thus Mr. Williams has by implication claimed not merely to have found bottom with his lead but also to have brought up highly important and hitherto unknown specimens from the ocean bed which have revolutionized his whole understanding of the great amphibian Man; in fact, I believe he has merely produced from the lower and less salubrious parts of the ship some interesting but unattractive biological organisms. And this, while admittedly useful from the point of view of sanitation and disinfection, can hardly provide us with the necessary materials for a twentieth-century pattern of Christian living. So much, then, in explanation of the title of this chapter, and I trust it will be clear that the noun which it contains is intended to express, in the metaphorical terms which Mr. Wil-

[1] p. xi.

31

liams and his colleagues have adopted, the subject which, as I see it, his essay discusses and not the essay itself.

Mr. Williams begins by inviting his theological contemporaries to learn a much needed lesson from the fate of their predecessors. In the sixteenth century they were forcibly and unwillingly fed with the astronomy of Copernicus and in the nineteenth century with historical criticism and natural science. In the end they swallowed the unfamiliar diet but not before great harm had been done. At the present day they are being confronted with a newer food still, that of Freudian psychology, and it is clear that Mr. Williams considers that they ought to be far more ready to take it into their systems than they are.

A few reflections suggest themselves at once. In the first place, Mr. Williams appears never to have heard of, or at any rate never to have taken seriously, any other modern psychologist than Sigmund Freud. Now, granted (as I am anxious to grant) that Christian moral theologians ought to pay a great deal of attention to the views and findings of modern psychology and even granted (as I am *not* prepared to grant) that Christian moral theology ought to be completely reconstructed in the light of it, it must still be recognized that Freudianism is only one of a number of schools of modern psychology and that its basic postulates are vigorously contested by a great many experts in the psychological field. The moral theologian who on the strength of Mr. Williams's soundings embarks in the vessel of Freud may very well find himself before long stranded on a sandbank while the Jungians and Adlerians and that large body of psychologists who refuse to fly the flag of any single master sail derisively past him down the stream. He will be acting as unwisely as would a Christian natural theologian who based his arguments for the existence of God upon the cosmological theories of Whittaker and Gamow in ignorance or contempt of the competing views of Hoyle and Bondi and of Lyttleton. (This has in fact happened and in very distinguished circles too! ) [2] It is in any case

[2] Cf. my *Christian Theology and Natural Science*, p. 149f.

simply not true that recent theologians have ignored the findings and insights of modern psychology, though it is true that
they have approached it with less one-sidedness than Mr.
Williams and with more discrimination. There are, for example, the profound symposia issued under the title *Études
Carmélitaines,* especially the volumes *Amour et Violence*
(1946) and *Trouble et Lumière* (1949). There is the massive
treatise of M. Roland Dalbiez *Psychoanalytic Method and
the Doctrine of Freud,* in which the author discriminates between psychoanalysis as a technique of investigation and a
therapeutic method (which he accepts) and as a philosophical
and psychological theory (which he rejects). There is the book
of Dr. Rudolf Allers *The Successful Error,* which, just
because it manifests a vigorous distrust of Freudianism on the
part of a professional psychologist, should make a Christian
theologian hesitate before committing himself unreservedly to
Freud. There is the balanced discussion *Psychoanalysis and
Personality* by Père Joseph Nuttin, which subjects the Freudian system and technique to a sympathetic and searching,
but, in the end, destructive examination. There is the penetrating study by the late Father Victor White, O.P., in *God
and the Unconscious,* in which the author, after a careful consideration of Freud and Adler, himself reaches a qualified
approval of the outlook of Jung; he quotes from Jung the
significant remark: 'The fact that many clergymen seek support or practical help from Freud's theory of sexuality or
Adler's theory of power is astonishing, inasmuch as both these
theories are hostile to spiritual values, being, as I have said,
psychology without the psyche.' [3] In view of such instances as
this—and it would be easy to add to them—it is really
astounding that Mr. Williams should accuse theologians of
neglecting modern psychology and should also identify modern
psychology with the system of Freud. It is, however, far more
alarming when we discover that Freud's great merit in the

[3] Jung, *Modern Man in Search of a Soul,* p. 263, cit. White, *God
and the Unconscious,* p. 47.

33

C

eyes of Mr. Williams is not concerned with his competence as a scientific psychologist at all, but with the purely subjective and psychological aspects of his techniques. 'When Freud attempted this [that is, the scientific] sort of construction in his more general non-clinical writings,' Mr. Williams admits, 'his arguments could be torn to shreds by any trained philosopher.' The scientist, we are told, 'is concerned to observe objective facts in the exterior world. Freud was concerned with people's subjective feelings.' Taking these two sentences together, we might conclude that in his non-clinical writings Freud had chosen a field of study in which he was not, in fact, very competent. But no; so far from having chosen to make an objective study of subjective phenomena, Freud was not concerned to make an objective study at all. 'Freud's genius . . . consisted in his discovery of a completely new system of explanation which was able to make sense of subjective feelings so far unexplained. The difficulty lies in the fact that the explanation cannot be apprehended merely by intellectual study.' What 'the difficulty' is we are not told, but we may suspect that it is the difficulty of knowing what exactly is meant by the words 'to make sense' in the previous sentence. However, we are told that

> there is something in it of Augustine's 'Believe that thou mayest understand.' As with Augustine, so with Freud, this is not a demand for irrational credulity (since such credulity is merely intellectual), but a demand that the risk be taken of opening oneself to a reality greater than is at present known to us. For Augustine the reality was God: for Freud the unknown self. For Augustine the way was prayer: for Freud analysis.

At this point we might reasonably expect Mr. Williams to flee shrieking 'Idolatry!', but it is a characteristic of some contemporary Christian writers that, so long as a man has the right attitude, they do not seem to think that it matters much what the object of that attitude is. In much the same way, in the famous Lady Chatterley trial, a highly placed Anglican dignitary expressed strong approval of D. H. Lawrence for his reverent and religious attitude towards sex, where a Christian of an earlier epoch would have seen this attitude as merely manifesting a violation of the First Commandment. But to return to Mr. Williams:

> Just as you cannot come to know God simply by making an academic study of prayer, so you cannot get to know your unknown self just by studying books about psycho-analysis. . . . That is why all schools of analysis insist that the analyst must himself be analysed as part of his training. It is like ordinands being made to pray.

It is difficult to see what is meant to be the practical force of this assertion. There is no difficulty in teaching any number of ordinands to pray, for the amount of individual attention that each will need is comparatively small, and in recent years more and more stress has been laid upon the desirability of the director playing a very minimal role in the spiritual life of the Christian. It is not altogether clear whether Mr. Williams means to imply that every Christian should undergo a course of psychoanalysis, though this would certainly seem to follow from the sequel of his argument; if this is implied, then in view of the length and expense both in labour and money of such a course, he would seem to be faced with an impossible task. We may notice that Mr. Williams rejects with vigour that suggestion that the necessary self-knowledge can be achieved by the use of drugs, mainly because he doubts on *a priori* grounds that so large a result can be achieved in so short a time. But we are also told, with reference to Mr. Aldous Huxley's claim that the drug mescaline provides 'a short-cut to the Beatific Vision,' that 'the question is whether awareness, a permanent increase of insight, can be manufactured by a drug, be it awareness of God or awareness of the self.' 'That these two are most intimately related,' Mr. Williams goes on, 'has been the unanimous opinion of Christian writers down the ages—"He is not far from each one of us: for in him we live and move and have our being" (Acts 17: 27f.).'

At this point, while recognizing with gratitude Mr. Williams's approval of Professor R. C. Zaehner's refutation of Mr. Huxley, we might observe that the important question is how these two awarenesses—the awareness of God and the awareness of the self—are related, and we might perhaps wonder whether the key might not be found in the Christian writers down the ages to whom Mr. Williams approvingly refers. In particular we have the teaching of St. Augustine, whom Mr. Williams himself mentions, and St. Bernard, whose Christian understanding of the principle *Gnothi seauton*— 'Know thyself'—has been made the subject of such a penetrating and illuminating study by M. Étienne Gilson.[4] But there is something frightening about Mr. Williams's remark about taking the risk of opening oneself to a reality greater than is at present known to us, for his immediately following remarks suggest that this is a good thing to do, whether that reality be the unknown self or God, and this seems to me to be highly questionable. And, although, in fairness to Mr. Williams, it must be added that he qualifies this assertion a good deal, he seems to me to be involved in considerable confusion.

'Our concern here,' he tells us, 'will be to discover how a man's knowledge of God and his attitude to God are affected by his growing awareness of what he is and how he functions as a psychic entity.' 'This,' we are also told (and here, I think, the subjectivity and relativism of the whole approach are revealed), 'of course will have important results in his subsequent statement of how any Christian doctrine is to be understood.' The really important passage, however, is the following:

> Freud and his successors, disciples or deviationists, have taught us how we can discover within ourselves a great deal of what was previously unknown to us, and such discoveries can tell us a great deal of how we think and feel about God. But the process is not simply an exercise in cerebration. It involves a costly surrender of what we imagine or hope or fear we are, to what in our fullness we really are.

[4] *The Mystical Theology of St. Bernard.*

36

What, however, is it that we really are? What is this reality of ourselves that we are to discover? Orthodox Christianity will reply that it is the truths that we are created by God and for God and exist in incessant dependence upon him, and that we have fallen away from him by sin and are redeemed to him by and in Christ. And once we are clear about this we can agree with Mr. Williams that we are called to something more than a mere intellectual acceptance of the statements about our real nature. As he says, 'It is only by doing the truth that we come to the light. It is only by actually making the journey that we can perceive the nature of the country.' But are we, or at least is Mr. Williams, clear about this? I very much doubt it. 'Unless we are prepared for this surrender,' he writes, 'the new understanding of human nature which Freud initiated will tell us nothing useful about that belief in God which is the material of our theology.' It is thus, apparently, to Freud, rather than to the saints of Christendom, that we are to look in order to understand what is involved for our life in our belief about God and our relation to him. 'In Christ,' Mr. Williams finely writes, 'we believe, God involved himself totally in our human predicament. How then, with regard to our own selves and psychic make-up, can we refuse to do the same?' For, he has just reminded us, 'the principle of Incarnation, as Christian theology understands it, is the principle of involvement.' 'And here,' we are somewhat surprised to be told, 'Freud'—not, be it observed, St. Augustine or St. Bernard, or even Christ himself, but Freud— 'pointed the way. For'—and now we are given a quotation from the leading Freudian analyst Dr. Gregory Zilboorg— 'he "promulgated the belief . . . that the psychological laws governing our unconscious, affective life are equally valid for all men, the mentally ill and the mentally healthy. . . . In other words, Freud opened the road for a proper psychological identification with the neurotic and psychotic . . . an identification based upon an actual psychological equation between ourselves and the mentally ill."' And this, Mr.

Williams goes on to say, 'is the involvement, the incarnation, and the cross of self-awareness. And this is why we are tempted to forsake Christ and flee, concocting for our flight the most convincing reasons possible. We cannot bear to put ourselves in the same class as the afflicted.'

With all respect and sympathy for Mr. Williams I must say that, as a description of the condition of the ordinary sinful Christian (or non-Christian, for that matter), this account seems to me to be thoroughly perverted, though in expressing this opinion of it I am no doubt, in Mr. Williams's view, merely manifesting the blindness and obstinacy of my sinful condition. No doubt there are pathological sufferers, who deserve our deep compassion and assistance, and to whom it is necessary to bring the recognition of their deranged condition. And no doubt none of us is psychologically the picture of health, any more than he is physically. But to say that the essence of sin consists in the refusal to recognize our affinity with the psychologically deranged is contrary to Christian belief, which holds that the essence of sin consists in our refusal to recognize our dependence upon God. Logically Mr. Williams seems to have fallen into the fallacy of defining the perfect in terms of the imperfect instead of the reverse, and, if the first step in our salvation consists in psychologically identifying ourselves with the mentally afflicted, in what will the first step in *their* salvation consist? It can hardly consist in identifying themselves with themselves. It may be the case, as Mr. Williams suggests, that if I have the habit of quarrelling with my friends it is because 'I am too frightened to receive into awareness the buried child within me, who is terrified of losing his own identity by parental domination or possessiveness,' but is quarrelsomeness always to be so explained, and when it is, is it to be cured simply by being 're-ceived into awareness'? When Mr. Williams writes 'Received into awareness, the child disappears. . . . It is thus that I pass through involvement with an alienated self, the cross and the passion, to the glory of the resurrection,' it is difficult not to feel that he has substituted salvation by a psychological technique for salvation by Christ.

After this preliminary discussion of the nature of sin in general, Mr. Williams proceeds to apply his theory to the question of our relationship to God. And here again he takes as typical a condition which seems to me to be very untypical and, when taken as typical, misleading. When, as is usually the case, I am more angry with a friend than reason would dictate, the reason is, Mr. Williams tells us, that I am making him stand for all the people who have treated me similarly since I was born. Similarly (but is it really similar?) I naturally feel a deep resentment against God because, although I have been told that he is my loving Father, I also believe him to be responsible for the ills which I suffer. However, I believe that theology can explain this wrongness of things, so I thrust my resentful feelings underground. By doing this I lose much of the vitality which otherwise I might use for my conscious purposes and expend much of the rest in keeping it underground. I thus fail to recognize the real trouble, which is that large areas of my being are as yet impervious to my critical reason and therefore attribute my irascible, depressed or nervous condition to plausible but quite false causes. After quoting in his support a passage from St. John of the Cross about the necessity of rejecting holy thoughts and feelings if one is to attain union with God—a passage whose precise relevance is difficult to see but which would seem to count as much against Mr. Williams's thesis as for it—Mr. Williams at last attempts to relate his psychological account to the Christian religion. Faith, he tells us, is the gift of God and cannot be fabricated by man. Psychological analysis cannot create it, nor can Bible-reading or attendance at Mass. Analysis, however, can, under God's providence, strip a man of what he mistakenly took to be an experience of God and show him that it was merely the experience of an earthly substitute. There is no suggestion that Bible-reading or attendance at Mass or any other religious exercise can effect this necessary spiritual therapeusis, so we are once again left wondering whether being psychoanalysed is a necessary part of the training of the Christian. Whatever the answer is, it is emphasized that the analyst's function is purely negative; he is merely cutting away the weeds which obscure the light of day. 'He does not claim to give that light. It comes, he would say, from within a man's own nature, or, as Christians would say, from God.' The alleged demoniacs in the Gospels, we are told, are simply men who have driven underground as blasphemous their reaction against the picture of God that the Old Testament has given them but have failed to keep it underground for very long, so that in the end it has burst out and destroyed their conscious personality. 'What Freud showed us was that every one of us, in some degree or other, has the same demon lurking inside us.' And what the Old Testament teaching did for the demoniacs in the Gospels, Mr. Williams tells us, has been done for many Anglicans by the exaggerated and repetitive penitential language of Cranmer's liturgy. How, I wonder, does he know all this, about either the demoniacs or the Anglicans?

To summarize the above discussion, with every desire to be sympathetic to Mr. Williams's effort to integrate Freudianism into the Christian system, I cannot feel that he has succeeded. For, first, he has ignored without discussion the very strong arguments against Freudianism which have been brought on purely empirical grounds by the rival schools of psychologists. Then, secondly, he has substituted for the Christian notion of sin the Freudian notion of psychological maladjustment, with the implication, never fully recognized, that some form of psychoanalysis should be applied to every one who is trying to live the Christian life. And, thirdly, his attempt at a later stage to Christianize a thoroughly secularist doctrine by introducing the notion of faith comes in far too late to be successful. However, the strongest criticism to which his treatment lies open will be more conveniently stated after we have considered his reassessment of moral values. And to this I shall now turn.

Mr. Williams begins by asserting that his reassessment of moral values is not a radical or basic one, though we may see reason to doubt this on closer examination. 'Christians,' he tells us, 'have always everywhere agreed that God is love, and that therefore generous self-giving love is the ultimate moral value. Where the reassessment is necessary is in our understanding of how and when we give ourselves and how and when we refuse to do so.' This would indeed seem to imply a fairly radical and basic reassessment, for it is equivalent to saying that the great saints and teachers of Christendom have been uniformly mistaken in their notions of the way in which a life of Christian commitment was to be lived and that nobody knew how and when to give himself until the time of Freud. Mr. Williams, however, continues, 'This makes it impossible to describe certain actions as wicked and others as good. For only I myself can discover in what actions I am giving myself and in what actions I am refusing to give.' To make these last two sentences mutually consistent we must assume that the actions referred to in the first sentence are those of other people, though we may note that if Mr. Williams's previous discussion is correct I can only make the necessary discrimination as regards my own actions after I have undergone the process of Freudian analysis which he has declared to be necessary for the attainment of self-knowledge. Leaving this difficulty aside, however, let us take Mr. Williams's words in their plain meaning and see what they imply. If it is, as he says, impossible to describe certain actions as wicked and others as good, then I cannot say that it is a wicked action to destroy millions of Jews, as Hitler did during the Second World War, or to rape a young girl or to torture a baby. I cannot suppose that Mr. Williams really believes this, so I can only assume that he is careless or confused in his use of words. There are, in fact, signs that he is not altogether clear about the commonplace text-book distinctions between single actions and classes of actions and between material and formal sin, but even if this is so it is not the whole story. For what Mr. Williams holds, and holds with passionate conviction, is that when I am faced with a moral decision I am to decide how to act, not my asking myself whether actions of such and such a type are morally right or wrong, nor by asking God to show me what it is his will that I should do, nor even by the utilitarian criterion of trying to assess the consequences for good and evil of the various courses open to me, but simply by discovering whether in this or that action I shall be giving myself or refusing to give, and this in spite of the fact that this discovery is one which we have already been told it is impossible to make without a protracted process of Freudian analysis.

To illustrate his thesis Mr. Williams gives two examples in the sphere of sexual ethics derived from recent films. In the first of these a young sailor, who has picked up a prostitute, is afraid and nervous, not because he thinks that fornication is wicked but because he distrusts his capacity for sexual union. 'He is a prey to destructive doubts about himself, not to moral scruples. The prostitute gives herself to him in such a way that he acquires confidence and self-respect. He goes away a deeper fuller person than when he came in. What is seen is an act of charity which proclaims the glory of God. The man is now equipped as he was not before.' In the second film a man is strongly attracted to young girls because of his fear of committing himself to an adult woman; when, however, a woman of his own age inspires him with enough confidence to sleep with her, he is made whole. 'And where there is healing, there is Christ, whatever the Church may say about fornication.' In Mr. Williams's interpretations, it is presumably the two women who are commended for having 'given themselves,' though on Mr. Williams's own principles it would appear that, even if they believe they are giving themselves they are in all probability hiding some much less creditable impulse under the mask of self-giving unless they have undergone the necessary process of analysis first. But what about the two men? The sailor, we are told, was timid and nervous not because he thought fornication was wrong but because he doubted his sexual capacity. Is a more old-fashioned moralist mistaken in suggesting that perhaps the young sailor might have become a deeper fuller person still (whatever those somewhat vague words imply) if he had become convinced of the wickedness of fornication? Has Mr. Williams, I wonder, any similar recipe for the man who is timid and nervous not because he thinks dishonesty is sinful but because he doubts his capacity successfully to rob a bank? And can the recipe be relied upon to work in any or every case, even in the sexual realm? (Of course, it did in the films because the film producers saw to that, but how often will it in real life?) Suppose the young sailor had not found himself to have acquired confidence and self-respect and to have become a deeper fuller person than when he went in. And suppose the other man found himself attracted to small girls as much as before. What will their fornication have done to them then? Will the appropriate response still be 'Glory to God in the highest,' because the two women 'gave them-selves'? I think it is considerations such as these which have led Dr. Henry Chadwick to write as follows, in a sympathetic but gently barbed discussion of Mr. Williams's essay: 'It remains an unconsidered question here whether, even if it was selfishness, cruelty, chicken-heartedness or plain discourtesy that deterred Joseph from accepting the urgent invitation of Potiphar's wife, he could have shown a true respect and love for her, and so fulfilled a distasteful duty according to the will of God, by consenting to the act.' [5]

There are indications that Mr. Williams is not too happy about all this. 'Freud,' he writes, 'showed us that evil consists of refusing to give through fear masquerading as morality. . . . Freud never taught that self-control of any kind led to illness, so long as people knew what they were doing. [What is meant by this characteristically vague phrase is nowhere made clear.] He did, however, conclude that most of us do

[5] 'Soundings,' a review-article in *Theology*, LXV (1962), p. 443.

not know what we are doing, and he claimed that God and his Law were devices to enable us to keep ourselves in as much ignorance as possible.' This, Mr. Williams admits, is often the case. The remedy is faith, but works often masquerade as faith, and this is the essence of sin. The doctrine of justification by faith is stated by Mr. Williams in highly Lutheran terminology, but there is nothing Lutheran about his highly original definition of faith. Faith, he says, could be defined as self-confidence, but this would suggest confidence in the limited superficial self and that would be the very opposite of faith. So perhaps we had better define faith as confidence in *life*. Faith, then, is 'a given (not acquired) certainty that the forces on our side are greater than the forces opposed to us. In Christian language, this is faith in God.' The identification made in the last sentence is indeed surprising, but it is typical of Mr. Williams's method that, instead of correcting the deficiencies of Freud's theories by the truths of Christianity, he simply applies Christian labels to the Freudian concepts and doctrines. Christian faith is surely very much more than the confidence that the forces on our side are greater than those opposed to us; after all, Hitler had that confidence and it could be consistent with the forces on both sides being purely mundane and impersonal. For Christianity, the faith that justifies is not faith in any sort of self, whether limited and superficial or profound and three-dimensional, but faith in God the Father and his Son Jesus Christ. However, in accordance with his definition Mr. Williams continues his diagnosis as follows:

> A man shows his lack of faith in God by his lack of faith in himself as flowing from God's creative act. The result is that he is incapable of trusting most of what he is. He trusts only a small part of himself—the self of which he is aware, the self which he can control and organize by conscious acts of will. . . . Hence the belief is generated that a man is no more than the self he knows. And it is from this identification of the known self with the total self that sin arises. . . . Examination [of the seven capital sins] will show that each of them

44

is due to the non-faith which leads me to equate myself without remainder with what I already know or feel about myself. This non-faith is a denial of God's creativity. It is an attempt to find security in the limited me of which I am aware instead of in the unlimited me which issues continuously from the Fount of Being, and of which I must be very largely unaware.

Now we may indeed be grateful for Mr. Williams's affirmation that faith involves a recognition of the fact that our being flows from God's creative act. And when Mr. Williams connects a man's lack of faith in God with lack of faith in himself as flowing from this act he at least suggests that faith in God and faith in oneself are not identical. However, in the sequel he seems to identify faith in God with faith in one's total self. There appears also to be a strange assumption that God's creative activity is operative in the unconscious levels of the human self but is not operative (or at any rate is not discernible) in the conscious levels. I am not trying to quibble and I am anxious to place the best possible construction upon Mr. Williams's assertions, even when they seem to me to be confused and obscure. But when I am told that the object of my faith and trust and the ground of my security is to be my total self—the 'unlimited me'—even when it is added that this unlimited me issues continuously from the fount of Being, I find it difficult not to conclude that I am being invited to have faith in myself as God's creature rather than in God who is my creator. And the natural issue of Mr. Williams's doctrine would seem to be, not faith in the Biblical and the traditional Christian sense, but the type of mysticism which finds its object in the soul itself.

I do not think I need examine the pages in which Mr. Williams deals *seriatim* with the seven capital sins and argues that each of them is due to failure to recognize the incompleteness of the superficial self; intermingled with much that seems to me to be debatable they contain a great deal that is penetrating and enlightening. The conclusion must, however, be noted; it is that 'the opposite of sin can only be faith and can never be virtue.' 'Faith,' we are again told, 'consists in the awareness that I am more than I know.' Freud 'showed that the sickness was due to the claim of the conscious self to be the whole man and thus to keep the rest in absolute subservience, alienated and unknown.' Freud thought that Christianity reinforced this tyrannical claim and Mr. Williams himself thinks that much, if not most, of Christianity does so. But what he describes as 'genuine Christianity' is on the contrary an unqualified protest against it. And it is here—and apparently only here—that he disagrees with Freud. In view of his readiness to set up his interpretation of the teaching of Christ against that of traditional Christianity this may be a suitable point to indicate certain dominical utterances to which Mr. Williams pays no explicit attention. 'If thy hand cause thee to stumble, cut it off. . . . If thy foot cause thee to stumble, cut it off. . . . If thine eye cause thee to stumble, pluck it out; it is good for thee to enter into the kingdom of God with one eye, rather than having two eyes to be cast into hell.' 'Every one that looketh after a woman to lust after her hath already committed adultery with her in his heart.' What is the Freudian reinterpretation of texts such as these?

Having criticized Mr. Williams as drastically as I have, I may reasonably be expected to indicate what I believe to be the basic defect in his exposition. It is, to state it quite briefly, that he seems to have lost sight altogether of both the beatific vision and sanctifying grace. That man is created for the vision of God and that his ultimate beatitude consists in achieving it seems to have fallen altogether out of Mr. Williams's consideration, which is entirely concerned with man's psychological integration, even when God is brought in as a necessary but somewhat pseudonymous agent in this process. I do not want in the least to depreciate the great services that modern psychological technique can perform in healing those who are mentally sick, though I should wish to stress the fact that Freud is not the only modern psychologist and that neither his theories nor his techniques are universally accepted by those best able to judge. But I protest most emphatically against Mr. Williams's assumption that the treatment of the mentally sick provides the guiding principles for the under-standing and conduct of the life of normal Christian people. He lays in fact far too much stress on the misery caused by lack of knowledge of oneself and far too little upon the joy conferred by the knowledge of God. The repudiation of the whole notion of progress in holiness which is expressed in his assertion that 'the opposite of sin can only be faith and can never be virtue' goes hand in hand with the assertion that 'when I attempt to make myself virtuous, the me I can thus organize and discipline is no more than the me of which I am aware.' And for all his talk about the necessity of self-abnegation Mr. Williams's discussion is concerned with self from start to finish; there is hardly a word about God, except as the ground of the unknown self, or any suggestion that people who are psychologically healthy will become what God wants them to be far more effectively if they keep their eyes on him, make use of the means of grace and try to serve him in their daily lives than if they reject the notion of virtue as pharisaical and rout about in their unconscious. In short, Mr. Williams's essay seems to me to provide about as plain an example as one could find of the fallacy of treating the normal as a special case of the pathological, and this seems to me to be true even of the moving pages towards the end of his essay in which he discusses the passion of Christ. I must add in conclusion a few comments on the passage in which he considers the place in Christian devotion of the Blessed Virgin Mary.

I do not think that I shall be suspected of wishing to diminish the honour that is due to the immaculate Mother of God, but I am greatly alarmed by the grounds on which Mr. Williams commends it. While recognizing the propriety of describing the First Person of the Blessed Trinity as the Father, he says that the figure of God the Father may become a destructive idol, on the grounds that 'a man's human experience is bound to colour his reactions to God as Father in those areas of his being not subject to the discriminatory control of his discursive reason.' It is suggested that the shadow of this idol has fallen in particular upon the penitential portions of the Communion Service of the Book of Common Prayer. Although he does not say so, presumably the Oedipus complex has cast its shadow on this part of Mr. Williams's argument, but in the case of most people it is sufficient to point out that human fatherhood, even at its best, is a very inadequate analogue for the fatherhood of God after whom all fatherhood in heaven and earth is named. Mr. Williams's point, however, is that we shall not avoid idolatry by simply ignoring our Lady, since we may well fall into idolatry in worshipping the Father if we have not been fortunate enough to enjoy the catharsis of Freud. So, he tells us, we are free to continue our investigations, and to ask what it is that, from the point of view of human feeling, accounts for the hold that the figure of our Lady has on Christians.

This very phrase 'from the point of view of human feeling' should warn us that once again Mr. Williams is inviting us to substitute psychology for theology [6] and is confusing the atti-

[6] Mr. Williams's extraordinary tendency to reinterpret theological statements as merely symptoms of the psychological condition of their authors is well illustrated by a passage in a recently published letter (*Theology*, LXVI (1963), p. 68). 'I agree,' he writes, 'that the Paul of the earlier epistles was incapable of accepting much of this world order, but that his ability to accept grew, until he was able to write in Ephesians of all things in heaven and on earth being gathered up in Christ. The intellectual form in which he clothed his incapacity to accept was his apocalyptic belief in the Lord's immediate return. But, in my view, such a belief was a rationalization of the apostle's incapacity to receive a great deal of his human nature.' Clearly, if Mr. Williams's technique is adopted it will become impossible to discuss the truth or falsehood of any assertions whatever, even of those which express the psychological reinterpretation. But for this last fact, I should be tempted to enquire what it was in Mr. Williams's own psychological history that led him to express his judgment about St. Paul! I do not think that it has usually been supposed that the Paul of the earlier epistles was unable to face up to his own nature, though I am interested to see that Mr. Williams accepts the apostolic authorship of Ephesians. Perhaps St. Paul became a deeper, fuller person at Corinth.

tude of religious devotion with its object. It is, no doubt, a
very bad thing to have an inadequate notion of the fatherhood of God, but, so long as it is God the Father whom one
is adoring, one cannot, in the strict sense, be said to be committing idolatry. And, *per contra,* if one gives divine honour
to a creature one will be committing idolatry, however
accurate one's notion of the nature of Godhead may be. Now
Mr. Williams accounts for the place which our Lady has held
in Christian devotion by asserting that 'in himself, God is no
more a father than he is a mother' and that 'our Lady . . . is
the symbol of that aspect of God's love which can be con-
veyed to us only by means of a feminine analogy.' While admitting that 'reliable statistics are impossible to obtain, for
few open their hearts sincerely to the social investigator,' Mr.
Williams asserts that 'it is conceivable that the absence in a
culture of a friendly woman-symbol (in other words, in atmo-
spheres where the fullness of God's love is not getting through)
makes it more difficult for men to grow into emotional
maturity.' Now I think it is, on theological and moral grounds,
a bad thing that our Lady should be deprived of the honour
that is due to her as the woman who, by her loving and
obedient *Fiat mihi secundum verbum tuum,* gave herself (in
a different sense from Mr. Williams's) to be the mother from
whom the Eternal Word took flesh for our salvation, but the
effect of such neglect on the emotional development of Protestants seems to me to be both secondary and debatable. To
quote Dr. Chadwick again, 'as there seem to be insuperable
difficulties in the way of establishing by sufficient empirical
evidence that, e.g., male homosexuality is in fact substantially
commoner in Protestant than in Roman Catholic and Orthodox societies, opinion on this subject is not likely to advance
beyond the expression of mere personal prejudice.' [7] But to
return to Mr. Williams.

'If the function of our Lady in transmitting to us that element of God's love which the father-symbol cannot convey

[7] art. cit., p. 443.

D

could be recognized,' he asserts, 'Protestants might be more willing to receive her.' I can myself think of nothing less likely and I should be very sorry if this were the case. I imagine that most Protestants would be outraged, and in my opinion they would be rightly so, at the suggestion that there was some important element in God's love which his name of Father could not convey and that our Lady had to be imported to convey it. It is significant that the only Christian thinker of note whom Mr. Williams can adduce for his thesis that there is motherhood in God is St. Anselm and, although this great saint is quoted as encouraging devotion to the motherhood of God, he is not quoted as urging this as a reason for devotion to our Lady. However, for Mr. Williams this is just where St. Anselm failed and this is why his new devotion had no future and was quickly forgotten; it is our Lady by whom the motherhood of God should be symbolized. Now Mr. Williams has such a tendency to substitute psychology for theology and ontology that it is difficult to know how many of his statements are meant to be taken as assertions of objective facts rather than as psychologically therapeutic imagery. But on the assumption of the former alternative I should wish to say, first, that the view that the fatherhood of God needs to be supplemented by the notion of motherhood is unscriptural, untraditional and devotionally dangerous; secondly, that the view that God's motherhood is transmitted to us in our Lady and is symbolized by her would, if taken seriously, lead directly to the giving of divine honour to a creature and would be idolatry in the strict sense (and not in the improper sense in which Mr. Williams uses it to imply the holding of an inadequate concept of the First Person of the Holy Trinity); thirdly, that Mr. Williams's remarks that Freud as a Jew was brought up in an entirely father-ridden religion, while 'in Christian devotion our Lady [but apparently not God the Father or our Lord Jesus Christ] has never been a forbidding figure,' would seem to leave the way wide open to that view of Mary as all mercy and the Father and

Christ as all justice which is perhaps the one really serious deviation to which devotion to our Lady has sometimes been subject. So long as our attitude to her is based upon the solid theological truth which was defined by the Council of Ephesus, that Mary is *Theotokos,* the Mother of God, we can give free rein to our love and gratitude towards her and can exalt her above the cherubim and seraphim without danger of idolatry or morbidity, but I tremble for the consequences if we are to take her as manifesting an aspect of the Godhead that the Persons of the Blessed Trinity are powerless to express. Even those extreme and unrepresentative Roman Catholic Mariologists who have argued that Mary has a primary and not merely a secondary part in the work of redemption, on the grounds that our Lord's human nature as male is incomplete unless it is supplemented by the femininity of Mary, have never gone quite as far as this. I would willingly agree that theological truths can have important psychological consequences, but Mr. Williams appears to take the opposite view that theological formulas are merely symbolic expressions of truths about human psychology, as is indicated by his extraordinarily banal remark that 'the Roman Church, in declaring our Lady to have been born without taint of original sin, gave expression in a theological idiom to what Freud later discovered in his consulting-room—the overwhelming influence for good or bad which a mother has upon her infant and child.'

It is painful to have had to make such drastic criticisms of an essay which clearly manifests a deep pastoral concern and a costing psychological experience on the part of its author. However, I cannot conceal my conviction that, in his desire to get beneath the deck of the ship with its somewhat showy and shoddy superstructure, this particular Leadsman has failed to take any soundings of the sea-bed at all but has, without understanding what he was doing, devoted himself to the unpleasant but, when properly performed, sanitary task of pumping out the bilge of the ship. His basic error, I would

51

suggest, is that, while saying a great deal about the *psychological* structure of man, as that is somewhat questionably conceived in the theories of Freud, he has overlooked the fact that man has any *ethical* structure at all or else has completely failed to distinguish between the two. For a serious discussion of the ethics of sex which might well have found a place in *Soundings* I would commend the article by one of the other Leadsmen, Mr. Howard Root, which appeared in October and November 1962 under the title 'Ethical Problems of Sex'; I will refer to it briefly in a footnote.[8] There

----

[8] See *Theology*, LXV (1962), pp. 408f. and 446f. This is not the place for a detailed discussion of Mr. Root's article and I shall merely mention one or two points which seem to me to be questionable, while commending warmly the article as a whole. (1) The use of the noun 'ideal' in reference to monogamous marriage seems to me to be misleading, as suggesting something which many may strive after but few attain, whereas its attainment, while demanding serious effort, is, as experience has shown, well within the capacities of the bulk of mankind. (2) Mr. Root writes: '[Christ] . . . said in one place that the Mosaic rules about divorce had been given because of the hardness of men's hearts. I hope I shall not be misunderstood if I say that, in a sense, the marriage ideal is also given because of the hardness of our hearts; i.e., because we need the order and direction it provides, and because without it we should not, *in our present state* [italics not in original], be able to find ourselves.' However, whatever Mr. Root may say, what Christ said was that 'in the beginning [i.e., in man's true nature as God has made it] it was not so,' since 'He which made them from the beginning made them male and female and said, For this cause shall a man leave his father and mother and shall cleave to his wife, and the twain shall become one flesh.' This certainly does not suggest that monogamous marriage is a concession to man's 'present state' of fallenness, nor does the picture of marriage as an analogue of the relation between Christ and the Church in Ephesians chapter five. I cannot help wondering whether Mr. Root has not failed to express his real meaning. (3) Mr. Root writes: 'The Christian moralist . . . is not committed to the view that all exercise of sex within marriage is right, any more than he is committed to the view that every exercise of it outside marriage is irredeemably wrong.' With the first half of this statement of course I agree; as regards the second half I am puzzled by the odd use of the adverb 'irredeemably' and I am not sure what precisely it means. If it means 'in all cases' then I think the statement is false if it refers to the objective nature of the act, but may sometimes be true if it refers to the subjective condition of the agents (*conscientia etiam erronea semper sequenda*); this is not, however, the normal meaning of 'irre-

is, however, another essay in the book itself, by Mr. G. F. Woods, on 'The Grounds of Christian Moral Judgment,' which, while less spectacular than Mr. Williams's, is free from his particular confusion, and to this I shall now turn.

deemably.' If it means 'unforgivably,' then clearly the statement is true, but it must be added that forgiveness involves the abandonment of the sin and not its continued commission ('Neither do I condemn thee,' said our Lord. 'Go, *and sin no more*'). There are great advantages in ethical discussion of adhering to the accepted terms of ethical theory and not introducing new ones without definition. With these reservations—which perhaps bear upon Mr. Root's forms of expression rather than upon the substance of his views his article seems to me to be admirable. The point which he makes about sex being serious but not to be taken too solemnly can be vividly illustrated by reference to the brilliant lectures on Christian Sex Ethics given recently by Dr. V. A. Demant at Oxford and shortly to be published in book form; it may be doubted whether such an extremely frank and direct exposition could have been delivered without either embarrassment or exaggeration but for the brilliant flashes of humour with which it was enlivened.

# CHAPTER III

# SOUNDINGS BY HAND

MR. G. F. WOODS opens his discussion of the Grounds of
Christian Moral Judgment [1] with the eminently sane observa-
tion that, although the minds of thoughtful and responsible
Christians are perplexed on quite a number of moral issues,
Christian moral perplexity is not a wholly new fact. Nevertheless, he tells us, the situation is a grave one and 'we cannot
meet the present challenge by moral dogmatism or moral
scepticism and we must be on our guard against accepting
superficial solutions which happen to be expressed in a contemporary terminology.' He deliberately avoids much traditional terminology, while refusing to condemn the traditional
vocabulary as obsolete. And his first concern is to show that,
both in secular and in Christian judgments, it is impossible to
avoid relying upon metaphysical grounds. Mr. Woods thus
faces his task in an attitude which is both courageous and at
the same time level-headed.

He begins his argument by insisting that moral judgments
are essentially irreducible, that is, that it is impossible to
identify a judgment that something *ought to be* the case with
a judgment that something *is* the case. He then asserts that it
is impossible for moral judgments to be made where there is
no moral agent. While agreeing with Mr. Williams (whom,
however, he does not mention by name) that we are not
always conscious of all the factors which have led to a moral
decision, he diverges from Mr. Williams in saying that 'it is our
duty, when we are made aware of these unconscious grounds,
not to despair of making well-grounded moral judgments but

[1] In the volume *Soundings* Mr. Woods's essay does not immediately follow Mr. Williams's. Their topics are, however, so closely
allied that there are advantages in discussing them consecutively.

actively to examine whether we can morally approve or disapprove of the factors which have unconsciously influenced our decision.' And he divides the conscious grounds of our moral decisions into two groups, those which concern our knowledge of what is the case and those which concern our knowledge of what ought to be the case. 'Our moral grounds are both factual and evaluative.'

Having thus clarified the nature of his task Mr. Woods then points out that three at least of the traditional grounds for Christian moral judgments have lost some of their former stability. First, the application of the historical method to the Bible has tended to undermine its authority as a repository of ethical instructions, though Mr. Woods rightly stresses that it has not been as destructive as is sometimes thought. Secondly, the whole conception of theological ethics, that is, the view that moral action consists in obeying the commands of God, seems to many people to be both impracticable and infantile. And thirdly, the evolutionary outlook of modern science has destroyed the idea that personal beings have a determinate nature in accordance with which it is their duty to live, so that the concept of Natural Law in the moral realm has been weakened: 'Natural law becomes a statement of what happens, not of what ought to happen.' However—and here Mr. Woods shows his level-headedness—the moral authorities which it has been attempted to substitute for the Christian moral tradition are themselves open to very serious criticism. While scientists as human beings have to make moral decisions, 'natural science can never of itself provide adequate grounds for moral decisions.' Here, of course, Mr. Woods is implicitly stating the case against the position defended in Dr. Waddington's book *The Ethical Animal*. Nor, he goes on to say, is any more help to be gained from contemporary Anglo-Saxon philosophy. 'It has concentrated upon an exact study of the use of language in moral discourse. The aim is to give an illuminating analysis of the way people talk when they are engaged in moral conversation.' What then of the existentialism of the Continent, with its view of man as a self-creative being, who has no unchanging essence and creates his standards in his actions? Logically, this might seem to involve sheer moral anarchy, but in fact, whether consistently or not, both Heidegger and Sartre distinguish between authentic and unauthentic living and set up the criterion of sincerity and integrity. However, Mr. Woods points out, this really gets one nowhere. 'A sheer emphasis upon sincerity and integrity, while supremely relevant in assessing praiseworthiness and blameworthiness, does not provide any clear ground for distinguishing between acts which are good and those which are bad. A man may quite sincerely do an act which is wrong. . . . Sincerity alone is not a sufficient guide for moral judgments.' Mr. Woods sums up this part of his discussion by comparing the thoughtful Christian of to-day to a navigator who has lost confidence in the reliability of his compass and the visibility and dependability of the heavenly bodies, and suggests that, as an interim solution, he may revert to the less sophisticated practice of taking soundings by hand, in the hope that this may lead him to more assured orientations.

Reverting to his earlier distinction between what we believe to be the case and what we believe ought to be the case, Mr. Woods maintains that the relevant facts of a moral case can only be known to those who are in some way involved in it and that their selection and assessment of the facts will be affected by their viewpoint. 'It follows that disputes about the form and content of moral cases are frequently disguised disputes about incompatible world views. In short there is no neutral account of the facts of a moral case which is uninfluenced by the standpoint, interests, and view of the world held by the observer.' It is, I think, quite clear that in saying this Mr. Woods is not suggesting that every man is free to make his own selection of moral facts and that there is no means of judging between such selections; quite the opposite. He explicitly distinguishes between what we believe to be the facts of the case and what are the facts of the case. His point is rather that, since what we believe to be the facts will depend upon our world view, it is practically essential,[2] if our belief about the facts is to be correct, that our world view shall be correct beforehand. And he makes a similar distinction when he turns to the second ground of our moral decisions, namely our belief as to what ought to be the case. 'We are conscious,' he writes, 'of a distinction between what we *believe* ought to be the case and what truly ought to be the case, irrespective of whether we recognize it to be so.' Thus Mr. Woods makes both a distinction and a subdistinction, and it may make for clarity at this point if we set these out in the following way:

I (*a*)   What *we believe to be* the case.

I (*b*)   What *is* the case.

II (*a*)   What *we believe ought to be* the case.

II (*b*)   What *ought to be* the case.

It is obvious that we are here poles apart from the moral relativism of Mr. Williams, with his assertion that it is impossible to describe certain actions as wicked and others as good. And Mr. Woods makes a further very important point which is central to his argument but which it would be easy to overlook. Behind all our moral formulations, he suggests, we have confidence that there *is* what *truly ought to be* the case, that is, in terms of the scheme that I have adopted, there is a fundamental identity between I (*b*) and II (*b*) or, in different language, that, whatever may be said about no amount of oughtness making an isness, ultimately what ought to be is grounded on what is. 'As long as we remain convinced that what truly ought to be cannot be inferior in being to the facts of the case which it criticizes, we are bound to seek some understanding of what truly ought to be in terms of what truly is.'

Turning now to consider the moral situation of the Christian, Mr. Woods insists that, both in his assessment of the

---

[2] I insert the word 'practically' because it is *logically* possible for a true conclusion to follow from false premises.

facts and in his view of what ought to be the case, the Christian will be directed by his specifically Christian beliefs. 'In assessing the facts of a moral case, the Christian . . . will view the case in the light of the Christian doctrines about God, the world and man.' And Mr. Woods vigorously defends the Christian from the accusation of dishonesty or peculiar bias. 'In so doing, [the Christian] is not gratuitously distorting the facts by introducing metaphysical considerations which are happily absent from all other accounts of the facts. He is being conspicuous because he is aware of his view of the world and because he is publicly acknowledging the view which he holds.'

And, just as his beliefs will guide his judgment of what the facts are, so will they guide his view of what ought to be the case. And here he has a wide and diversified range of material, comprising the image which he has of Christ's life and teaching and his idea of Christ's mind and spirit, the general impression of the Christian way of life which is shown in Christian history, the classic catalogues of Christian virtues, and more general formulations in terms of rules and law and standard. Mr. Woods rightly points out that the discovery, formulation and use of these Christian moral principles are all highly mysterious. I presume he has in mind here the oversimplified attitude to moral behaviour which is suggested by the more plantigrade type of manual of moral theology, for which the model of moral decision would seem to be that of an electronic computer which was programmed with the principles of Christian morality and which, when the facts of any particular moral situation were fed into it, would apply the principles in a purely logical way to the facts and triumphantly produce the detailed specifications of the appropriate moral action. (In fact, of course, the elaboration in moral theology of such highly special doctrines as that of Probabilism show that such a model, even as an ideal, would be foreign to the nature of moral theology itself.) Mr. Woods pertinently remarks that in some cases the principles may seem to be so wide as to offer virtually no guidance at all, but he points out that in most cases the principles which are used are neither extremely general nor extremely particular, and he makes the stimulating suggestion that 'we need more formulations of such principles as a guide for bodies of Christians who pass their daily lives in broadly similar occupations.' 'We need,' he writes, 'fresh principles of situational ethics which are easily seen to be broadly relevant to the types of situation in which men find themselves in contemporary society. Such principles would never cover all cases but their formulation and use would sharpen and assist the Christian conscience in making well-grounded moral decisions.'

In the final section of his essay Mr. Woods takes up his previous assertion that 'there is a deep Christian conviction that somehow there is a realm in which what ought to be is what is.' This, he makes plain, is not just a matter of courageous existential decision in defiance of the facts but of conviction about what is true. 'It is a matter, not of moral courage, but of the truth.' Mr. Woods fully recognizes the difficulty which many modern people have in believing in a personal God, and he stresses the duty which lies upon Christians of removing any avoidable impediments. Rather along the lines of his excellent book *Theological Explanation* he outlines an apologia for theism starting from our own moral experience, our own awareness of 'the mysterious tension between what we are and what we ought to be,' our 'experience of a unified personal being in which moral unity is not fully attained.' 'In momentary acts of sheer Christian charity,' he writes, 'we know that this tension is overcome. From these mysterious experiences of our own personal being we may draw analogies which may go some way in assisting us to think of the being of God in whom there is no tension between what is and what ought to be.'

Thus, Mr. Woods concludes, however disappointing this may be to readers for whom the traditional structure of Christian doctrine has ceased to be a living faith, there is an essential bond between Christian morality and Christian doctrine. He is explicit upon the need of restatement and retranslation of Christian doctrine in terms which will both be intelligible and appear relevant to modern men and women. But he is, I think, quite clear that, however greatly the traditional formulations need recasting, their essential content must remain the same. And although the needed reformulation may take a long time, Mr. Woods is plainly convinced that practical Christians are not in fact deprived of the necessary means of living in the Christian way of life. This is a courageous and challenging assertion, and it is well that it should be made at a time when it is only too easy for Christians to plead the alleged fluidity of the doctrinal situation as an excuse for the abandonment of the traditional pattern of Christian moral behaviour and when there are writers on Christian morals who seem only too anxious to encourage them to do so.

Mr. Woods, as we have seen, modestly describes his method as that of taking soundings by hand. 'These,' he writes, 'are not infallible but they may be the start of more assured orientations.' In this, I think he is right and, although his essay has attracted less attention than those of some of his fellow-Leadsmen, I believe it will in the long run be found to be one of the most valuable. I must confess that, while reading both this and his previous essay in the volume, I have more than once found myself asking the question *Qu'allait-il faire dans cette galère?* And it is with no lack of appreciation of an essay which does about everything that could be done in the space available that I mention one or two relevant problems on which I wish he had had the space to follow out his suggestions.

First, while Mr. Woods admits that he is writing as a Christian for Christians (and that he may disappoint some of his readers in doing this), I wonder whether, while still writing from a Christian standpoint, he could have said a little more about the nature of man simply as man. He rightly points out that the idea of man as a being with a determinate nature,

and thus as having a definite moral structure, has been under-
mined as a practically effective force by the empirical attitude
of modern science and by the development of evolutionary
theory. It has, however, been recognized by many scientists
who are not Christians that there is a lot to be said for the
view that, even on purely scientific grounds, an organism
which was capable of rational thought and behaviour would
have to possess, in their broad outlines, the physical, psychological and social structures that characterize man as we know
him; Sir Julian Huxley is perhaps the best known supporter
of this view. Again, I should like to have seen some further
discussion of the concept of the natural moral law, which Mr.
Woods admits is still very influential, although it has lost
some of its effectiveness. In particular, I would suggest that
considerable advance might be made if a clear distinction was
drawn between two different things which both appear to be
denoted by the term 'natural law' and are frequently confused. The first meaning is that of the moral law in so far as
it is discernible by man's natural powers without the aid of
the Christian revelation; the second is that of the moral law
in so far as it is concerned with man's life as a member of
human society in this world, in abstraction from his supernatural end in the beatific vision and from that life of grace
which is a preliminary and an anticipation of it. However,
these may be some of the 'other subjects' which, in the
Editor's words, 'might have been included and that another
group of essayists might have taken up.'

## CHAPTER IV

## NEW LEADS FOR OLD

It is a remarkable feature of the volume *Soundings* that, of the eleven essays which it contains, only two are devoted to strictly doctrinal subjects, those of Mr. Montefiore and Dr. Lampe, on Christology and the Atonement respectively. There is nothing on God as the Eternal Trinity or as the Creator of the World, nothing on the Holy Spirit, nothing on Grace or the Church or the Sacraments, if we except the brief note on Authority and Liberty in the Church which Dr. Vidler has appended to Mr. Sanders's essay on the New Testament. Nevertheless, the two doctrinal subjects which are included are of central importance and it will be of great interest to see what are the aspects of them which, in the opinion of their authors, are (to quote the Editor's words in his Introduction) not yet being faced with the necessary seriousness and determination. First, then, to consider Mr. H. W. Montefiore's essay, 'Towards a Christology for To-day.'

Mr. Montefiore begins by quoting Matthew 22: 42, 'What think ye of Christ?' and continues by saying 'There can hardly be a more obvious question than this for any Christian to face; for our Christianity stands or falls by our answer.' It is not, I think, mere cavilling to point out that in understanding the text as he does, to mean 'What think ye of Jesus?', Mr. Montefiore is in fact already assuming an answer which might seem to need more attention than he gives it, namely the answer 'Jesus is the Christ.' For, as we have only to look at the context in order to see, when our Lord put to the Pharisees the question 'What think ye of the Christ; whose son is he?', he was not asking them 'What do you think about me?', but 'What do you think about the Messiah?' It is not so much this question that, in Mr. Montefiore's words, 'challenges us to formulate our deepest convictions and to declare our fundamental loyalties' as the question which the Lord had previously put to his disciples, 'Who do you say that I am?', and which drew from Peter the spontaneous confession 'Thou art the Christ, the Son of the Living God.' It is strange that Mr. Montefiore should overlook this point, for it appears later on in his essay that he is very much concerned to get back behind the conceptual language of Greek theology to the dynamic language of primitive Jewish Christianity, and the fact that we have now come to use the word 'Christ' as a mere name, synonymous with 'Jesus,' is itself the result of that inability of Gentile Christianity to cope with the Jewish notion of the Messiah which led in the end to the Definition of Chalcedon whose reinterpretation Mr. Montefiore demands. It led also, of course, to the fact that the word 'Christology' itself has come to mean, not 'doctrine about the Messiah,' in which sense any Jew might be said to have a Christology even if he repudiated our Lord as an impostor, but simply 'doctrine about Jesus,' in which sense we can have a treatise on Christology which hardly discusses his Messiahship at all.

Now, whatever judgment we may ultimately form of Mr. Montefiore's conclusions, it is clear that the task which he set himself is that of reinterpreting the traditional doctrine of the Church about Jesus and not of substituting a different and more 'up-to-date' doctrine for it. For not only, as we have seen, does he accept the identification of Jesus with the Jewish Messiah to an extent which has led him unconsciously to misinterpret a New Testament text, but he explicitly begins his main discussion by endorsing the Christological definition of the Council of Chalcedon. 'The task of Christology,' he writes, 'is to reduce the mystery of Christ's person to propositional form. Any attempt to formulate a Christology will properly start with the Chalcedonian Definition, for here was an authoritative attempt by an Ecumenical Council of the Church to put into words and into concepts the mystery of Christ's person.' And he then quotes the Definition *in extenso*.

With the substance of these statements I heartily agree, though it may be relevant to note that, if we are to use words in their strict theological sense (and there is much to be said for this in a theological discussion), Christology would seem to be concerned not only with the mystery of his *person* but with the duality of his *natures;* and the mystery of his *person* might seem to have been the concern of Nicaea rather than of Chalcedon. However, Mr. Montefiore seems to use the word 'person' in a wider and looser sense, for he goes on to tell us that the carefully worded clauses of the Definition must not be despised for their apparent remoteness from the earthly life and ministry of the historical figure of first-century Palestine, since 'they were formulated not to describe his life but to define his person.' And Mr. Montefiore defends them on the ground that 'they were intended to safeguard three vital dogmas which seemed to be imperilled: the Unity of God, the Divinity of Christ and the Unity of Christ's Person' (here 'person' appears to be used in the strict theological meaning).

Mr. Montefiore thus stands before us as a supporter and not an opponent of the Chalcedonian Definition, and as I shall have later on to offer some rather sharp criticisms of his argument it is only fair to emphasize this point. He does indeed make it plain that his endorsement of Chalcedon is linked with a conviction of its limitations, but I see nothing to quarrel with in this. Has not Dr. Hans Küng, writing with all the respect for tradition which his Roman allegiance lays upon him, reminded us that even the most solemn dogmatic definitions, for all their freedom from error, may not always have been formulated in the ideally best way and are always conditioned by the limitations imposed upon them by the circumstances of their time? [1] But we must now attend to the particular difficulties about the Definition which Mr. Montefiore believes that it raises.

His first point I find very puzzling. It is that, by saying in

[1] *The Council and Reunion*, p. 166f.

positive terms that Jesus is perfect or complete in both manhood and godhead instead of adopting the negative form
'there is nothing pertaining to complete godhead or to complete manhood which is lacking in Christ,' the definition
assumes that we know the nature of godhead and manhood.

Now, objects Mr. Montefiore, the nature of God is, as the
scholastics themselves insist, beyond our human compre-
hension. We only know God by his effects; and, 'if we had
really known the nature of God, there would have been no
need of an Incarnation to reveal him to us.' (We might
strengthen the objection by remarking that, if God was
totally and necessarily unknowable by a finite mind, he could
not be revealed to us by an Incarnation or anything else.)
Nor, the objection continues, do we know the nature of manhood apart from Christ, because, first, our growing knowledge
of evolution prevents us from drawing an absolute line between man and the higher mammals and, secondly, the picture
of man which emerges from the natural and human sciences
is still confused and unintegrated. Now, apart from the
relevance or irrelevance of the references to the sciences just
mentioned, I find it difficult to see the force of the objection
as a whole. Even if our knowledge of the nature of both God
and of man was minimal, so that, for example, we knew
nothing whatever about God except that he was the uncon-
ditioned ground of the world's existence and nothing whatever about man except that he was the kind of being that we
ourselves are, it would still make sense to say that Jesus was
perfect God and perfect man, and unless we could say it we
could not make use of the figure of Jesus to enlarge our concepts of Godhead and manhood. Dr. Montefiore himself remarks that 'if we had really known the nature of God, there
would have been no need of an Incarnation to reveal him to
us.' We might comment that, unless we could significantly say
that Jesus was God, the Incarnation itself would not reveal
him. And Mr. Montefiore himself tells us that without real
knowledge of God's activity apart from Christ we should have

no means of recognizing the fullness of divine activity in Christ. So I am not sure whether in fact he thinks that there is very much substance in this objection.

A more serious objection which Mr. Montefiore adduces is that the language of substance, nature, *prosopon* and *hypostasis*, which the Chalcedonian fathers used, was, although they did their best with it, sub-personal; and impressive sentences are quoted from G. L. Prestige and William Temple to this effect. It may not be altogether a quibble to point out that *prosopon* is in fact the Greek for 'person,' and I think it is altogether relevant to stress that it is precisely because of its concern to maintain that Christ *is* a person (and is *one* person and not two) that, when it refers to Christ's human *nature,* the Definition uses language that is 'impersonal' or, if the phrase be preferred, 'sub-personal.' And Mr. Montefiore is really not being fair to the Definition when he says that 'Manhood and godhead are not comparable natures to be set side by side as in the Definition.' For first the Definition does not just set the manhood and the godhead 'side by side'—that would be sheer Nestorianism; it says that they both concur into the one Person. And secondly, it does not treat them as 'comparable,' for it says that Christ was 'begotten of the Father before all ages as regards his godhead' and was begotten 'in the last days . . . of Mary the Virgin Mother of God as regards his manhood'; and there can hardly be two derivations more different than a derivation in eternity from the Creator and a derivation in time from a creature. Mr. Montefiore goes on to remark that the particular philosophical tradition which underlies the Chalcedonian Definition is outmoded to-day, and quotes Dr. W. R. Matthews to the effect that the tendency of modern thought is to evolve dynamic concepts. Now this may be true of philosophy at the beginning of the century, when it was still largely under the influence of Hegelian idealism, but it would certainly not be true of the fashionable linguistic philosophy of to-day, though it might perhaps be true in a qualified sense of some types of Continental existentialism. Nevertheless, I think it would be a valid comment upon the Chalcedonian Christology that it gives an analysis of the *product* of the Incarnation where, for example, the Nicene Creed gives a description of the *process:* 'Two natures concurring into one person,' in place of 'the only-begotten Son of God, who came down from heaven and was made man.' However, it is fair to remember that Chalcedon did not only put out its own definition but also endorsed the Niceno-Constantinopolitan formulas. It should be added that there is not necessarily anything more Christian or religious about 'dynamic' concepts than about 'static' or 'substantial' ones; for 'power' (*dynamis*) can very well be impersonal, as every consumer of electricity knows, and *substantia* can very well be personal, as in the famous definition of Boethius: *Persona est rationalis naturae individua substantia.* It is, I think, in recognition of this fact that, in a footnote to a sentence which I am just about to quote, Mr. Montefiore writes: 'The phrase "dynamic function," while it may suggest impersonal mechanism, is used here in the sense of activity and energy proper to persons.' But this will bring us to the third objection which he adduces to the Chalcedonian formula. 'The biblical revelation,' he writes, 'is not expressed in philosophical terms, because the Jews did not think philosophically. They were concerned not with ontological definition but with dynamic function and with personal relationship.' A basic concept of both Testaments is that of Covenant, and, we are told, the New Testament, in its witness to Christ, is concerned primarily with what Christ did for men and with the difference that this makes to our relations with God and with each other. We shall see the implications of this in the sequel.

Mr. Montefiore begins his positive work of reinterpretation by taking as his starting-point the testimony of Jesus to himself as it is contained in the synoptic Gospels. There, he tells us, 'we find Jesus speaking of himself as a man, as a prophet, and as more than a prophet; as the One whose ministry was to be the prelude to the inauguration of God's Kingdom on earth. Jesus knew himself to be the Son of his heavenly Father: he described himself as Lord and as Son of Man. Negatively, he did not describe himself as God: indeed, he even seems explicitly to have denied this [Mark 10: 18].' Mr. Montefiore thus stands between the conservative position which would take the Fourth Gospel as being as reliable an authority as the synoptics for the *ipsissima verba* of our Lord and the liberal position which would take the dominical utterances in the synoptic gospels themselves as mainly the product of the mythopoeic activity of the primitive Church. It would be unreasonable to expect a reasoned justification of the precise position taken up by Mr. Montefiore in the space at his disposal, and in any case one of his fellow-Leadsmen, Mr. Sanders, has devoted his essay to the subject. It may be well, however, in the interest of clarity to take note of the point and also to recognize that it is Mr. Montefiore's purpose to reinterpret the Christology of the Bible and the Church in terms congenial to the present-day man or woman and not, except by implication, to argue either that the synoptic account of Jesus' teaching is reliable or that the claims which he made for himself were true. That is taken for granted, but unless this is realized I fear that some of the readers for whom the book is intended may feel that Mr. Montefiore has slipped out to sea under cover of darkness and left them standing on the quayside.

Mr. Montefiore makes it clear that his adoption of the synoptic tradition as basic is due not only to a desire to get back to the sources but also to a conviction that the Biblical outlook is closer than that of the Fathers and of Chalcedon to the dynamic categories which, rightly or wrongly, he believes to be congenial to the contemporary mind. Unlike some of our 'Biblical' theologians, however, he asserts that the Biblical interpretation of Christ is neither infallible nor normative for dogmatics, but he does hold that 'a Christology which is expressed in terms of functional and personal relationship

68

rather than in ontological categories means a return to the biblical perspective.' As he sees the matter, what Greek theology did was to turn three basic biblical images into philosophical concepts. Son of Man and Son of God became *vere homo* and *vere deus* respectively; Logos, after an unsuccessful philosophical career, ended up as merely another name for Christ. He might have added that, even in the New Testament itself, Christ was becoming another name for Jesus.

Mr. Montefiore recognizes that he is not the first person who has 'translated' orthodox Christology into contemporary terms, and he is very conscious of the danger that, in doing this, the translator may distort the substance of his material. Hegel, Ritschl and Schleiermacher adopted the regulative categories of the idea, of value and of feeling respectively, Thornton that of organism, Gore and his followers those of philosophical idealism, and Bultmann those of existentialism. To-day, however, the task is made more difficult by the general distrust among philosophers of metaphysical systems of any kind. Mr. Montefiore is nevertheless not prepared, as are many of his contemporaries in the theological world, to abandon metaphysics and reinterpret the Christian formulas as simply rubrics for liturgy, recommendations of ethical behaviour-patterns or incantations for psychotherapeutics. He does, indeed, very sensibly maintain that there is no need to declare a moratorium on either Christian faith or Christian worship or Christian morals until the theologians have cleared up their difficulties. It is the intellectuals who are in the impasse, not the Church. Nevertheless, the impasse is serious and needs to be removed and its effect upon the Church is serious, for, while faith is faith and not understanding, faith nevertheless seeks to understand. And, whatever the climate of modern philosophy may be, this means a recovery of metaphysics. 'For theology,' writes Mr. Montefiore, 'metaphysics are essential, if theology is not to preside over its own suicide.' Here I believe he is entirely right, and I would suggest that the recovery of a genuinely metaphysical outlook in theology might well turn out to be the preliminary to its recovery in philosophy. We have now to examine Mr. Montefiore's soundings in order to see how far they get us on our course.

Following up his earlier approbation of dynamic and personal categories, he notes that Dr. Tillich has proposed the substitution of the categories 'eternal God-man-unity' or 'eternal God-Manhood' for 'divine nature,' on the ground that these replace a static essence by a dynamic relation. (I wonder, incidentally, whether there is a reflection of Soloviev's notion of 'god-manhood' here.) Mr. Montefiore commends Tillich for grounding his Christology on ontology rather than psychology, though he condemns the extreme scepticism of Tillich's attitude to the historical Jesus. Oddly, he fails to comment upon an equally unsatisfactory feature in Tillich's project, namely that in proposing to substitute 'eternal God-man-unity' for 'divine nature' Tillich is proposing to substitute monism for Christian theism. However, Mr. Montefiore finds greater usefulness in Dr. W. R. Matthews's concept of human personality as a 'moving pattern of activity' and his employment of this to relate Jesus to God. This, he maintains, is in fullest accord with the Biblical outlook, concerned with divine activity rather than with being; he has already quoted Dom Gregory Dix and Dr. Cullmann on this point. And he proposes to state his 'Christology for to-day' entirely in terms of divine activity and without any reference to divine nature or being; his key-concept is that of 'the pattern of divine activity.' And it is at this point that he seems to me to go badly astray.

I cannot help doubting whether, in any case, the modern man will find his understanding and his will reacting more eagerly to talk about 'the pattern of divine activity' than to the language of the Nicene Creed, but my objection lies deeper than this. It is that Mr. Montefiore's conceptual scheme makes it impossible for him to distinguish between views between which the conceptual scheme of traditional theology is perfectly well able to distinguish, largely because it was elaborated for this purpose. Thus he writes: 'Instead of defining the Essential Trinity of three Persons, we must content ourselves with the experience of the divine activity in three modes.' In other words, we must content ourselves with being unable to discriminate between orthodox trinitarianism and Sabellianism. I must make it plain that I do not in the least suspect Mr. Montefiore of being a Sabellian but only of being unable to say whether he is one or not, and this seems to me to reveal a glaring inadequacy in the linguistic technique which he asks us to accept. For the first requisite for any conceptual or terminological scheme is that it shall have different words to apply to objects which are different from one another in important respects. Mr. Montefiore is in fact in very much the position of a man who has attempted to translate an English work on arithmetic into one of those primitive languages in which, so we are told, the only numerals are 'one,' 'two,' 'three' and 'many.' He will be unable to distinguish between what we call 'six' and 'forty-five' and will be in grave difficulties if he makes use of his translation when buying seats for the theatre or shoes that will fit his feet. It is, I think, significant that, although Mr. Montefiore makes some attempt to show that his terminology will serve us as well as that of Chalcedon, he never tries to show that it is able to make distinctions of importance which Chalcedon is unable to make. But this is one of the things which, if it represented a real advance in theological understanding, we should expect it to do.

The consequences of Mr. Montefiore's proposal are indeed far-reaching, for, unlike St. John, he finds himself able only with great reservations to say that God is Love, since that involves speaking about God's nature. And here he introduces, though without comment, a new argument which needs attention. We know nothing about God's being and nature, he tells us, except that God is transcendent over us. However, since God's action must be a revelation of his nature, and since God *acts* as a God of love, we may be allowed to say that his inmost nature is love, so long as we remember that saying this does not add anything to our knowledge. Now Mr. Montefiore really ought not to dismiss the whole question of the divine transcendence in this casual way, especially when his fellow-Leadsman Mr. Woods has contributed a very good essay to the book on this very subject. It is also relevant to remark that traditional Christian thinkers have developed an elaborate doctrine of analogy in order to deal with this kind of problem. I cannot, however, wonder that, in spite of his downright declaration that 'we shall not speak about the being and nature of God himself,' he wavers a sentence or two later, for he has by implication dismissed as irrelevant Basil on the Holy Spirit, Augustine on the Trinity and practically the whole of the thought of the Greek and Latin Fathers. However, he rapidly recovers himself and repudiates even so moderate a statement as that of C. C. J. Webb that there is personality in God. 'We cannot go so far even as that. We must content ourselves with saying that God works in a personal way.'

Now this last statement merits examination, for as it stands it is highly paradoxical. It goes further than asserting that personal activity is experienced by us; for it attributes this activity to God. *God* acts in a personal way. We are, however, prohibited from saying that God is a person (or a trinity of persons). But why? Well, partly, as we have just been told, because of the divine transcendence, although if we can say *nothing* about God's nature it is difficult to see who it is to whom we are attributing this personal activity when we say that *God* is acting in a personal way. Behind this introduction of the divine transcendence, there lies, however, Mr. Montefiore's basic assertion that, if we are to be true to the Bible, we must speak in terms of action and not of being. Now it is of course true that the Bible speaks a great deal about divine action, but one does not need to be a metaphysician to hold that the way in which any one acts is an indication of

the kind of person that he is. 'In the Bible,' writes Mr. Montefiore, 'we find that God is not so much he who is as he who
acts.' I am not clear as to the force of the words 'not so much'
in this sentence. If Mr. Montefiore meant that God is *not* he
who is, I imagine he would have said so. He must therefore
presumably mean that the Old Testament talks more about
God's action than about his being. This may well be so, and
it is perfectly compatible with God being *both* he who is *and*
he who acts, and with his activity being a clue to his nature.
After all, this is true of the activity of finite beings, and it is
difficult to see why it should not be true of God. If a man
said to us 'I cannot go so far as to say that my wife is a
person; I must content myself with saying that she works in
a personal way,' we should think he was speaking very oddly
and might suspect that he was a highly conscientious sur-
vivor from the wreck of logical positivism, or else that he was
an avid reader of science fiction and was afraid that he might
have married a well-constructed robot by mistake. And I
think that the man of the present day, when Mr. Montefiore
says to him 'I cannot go so far even as saying that God is a
person; I must content myself with saying that God works in
a personal way,' is unlikely to feel that at last the Christian
religion is being presented to him in a way that he can understand and, on the strength of it, rush to offer himself for
baptism. I think he is more likely to recoil in dismay and flee
into the arms of Dr. Waddington or of Chalcedon. I wonder,
however, whether Mr. Montefiore is really being loyal to his
own intention in some of his more extreme expressions; for
there are clear signs that he switches from comparisons to
denials in a way that is logically very puzzling. Thus, just
after the sentence quoted, he writes (the italics are mine):
'God was active in Christ *not primarily* to show himself to
man but to do something for man. . . . The New Testament
is *primarily* concerned not with existence but with salvation.'
And then, apparently under the impression that he is either
repeating himself in other words or else stating a logical con-

sequence, he immediately adds: 'Christ did *not* come to make us divine, *but* to bring us to God.' 'Not X so much as Y; therefore Y and not X'—I think a good deal of the writing of modern Biblical theologians will be seen on examination to follow this peculiar canon of inference.

Mr. Montefiore passes on to trace and interpret the 'pattern of divine activity' in the life of Jesus, so far as it can be recovered from the Gospels. He gives a truly moving account of the ministry of the Lord and of the way in which his disciples were brought to 'recognize in him One who in some way was to be identified with him who brought the Jews out of Egypt and who fashioned the stars and the earth.' But, like Mr. Williams, he tends so much to interpret our fallen condition in psychological terms that we are left with the impression that either every one must be psychologically deranged or else there are some healthy souls who have no need of salvation. Furthermore it must be noted that Mr. Montefiore clearly regards the physical historicity of both the virginal conception of our Lord and his Resurrection as irrelevant to the Christian religion. 'The Resurrection appearances are not dissimilar in form from other paranormal phenomena of the same general kind. But they are unique in meaning. . . . Thus God, after Jesus' death, communicated his triumph to his friends and enabled them and others to share in it, just as, by a different mode, he still communicates that triumph to us, that we too may share in it.' There is in fact a general reinterpretation of the supernatural events of the Christian religion as being 'symbolic' in a way which is undefined but which certainly seems to look upon both their factual and their supernatural character as doubtful or irrelevant. Thus, 'as the Virgin Birth symbolizes the beginning of the moving pattern of activity focused in a personal life, so the Ascension marks its completion': does this, I wonder, mean, in Chalcedonian terms, that the hypostatic union was dissolved at the Ascension, or is this one of those questions that cannot be significantly formulated in the new translation? 'The Second Coming symbolizes the hope that in the end the whole world will manifest the same pattern of divine activity as perfectly as it was manifested in the human person of Jesus.' Yes, but will this hope be realized? Will Jesus come again with glory to judge both the quick and the dead? Will his kingdom have no end? And does the word 'was' imply that the pattern is no longer manifested or that Jesus is no longer a human person? Why 'was,' rather than 'is'? I ask these questions not because I want to be tiresome but because they seem to me to be really important and because it seems to me to be at least doubtful whether Mr. Montefiore's proposed Christological categories provide a medium in which they can be either asked or answered. And one of the consequences of treating everything in the Gospels after the deposition in the tomb as 'symbolic' is that so far as historic facts are concerned the incarnate life of the Son of God finishes on the Cross. 'His ministry led up to and found its climax in his death. The Cross formed its focus and culmination.' There is no suggestion of the theme which is so triumphantly expressed in the paschal liturgies and in the teaching of St. Paul in Romans about baptism, that Christ's passion, death and resurrection together form one great mystery of redemption and re-creation, through which men and women pass when they die with Christ and rise again with him as members of his mystical and eucharistic body the Catholic Church. We are told indeed that 'inasmuch as the body of believers (the Church) is identified with the work of Jesus, they become the Body of Christ, and the same pattern of spiritual energy is manifested in them as it was in Jesus'; what we are not told is whether they are incorporated into the human nature which the Son of God assumed from his mother, for it is altogether unclear whether he is still considered to be man or not.

In the final section of his essay, in which Mr. Montefiore looks back upon the achievements of his discussion, there are signs that he is not too happy about it He quotes Dr. Matthews as admitting that his 'moving pattern' conception cannot adequately describe the nature of human personality and still less the meaning of the Incarnation, but he nevertheless holds that it can shed a ray of light upon the present Christological impasse. And, in accordance with his avowed purpose of restating and not supplanting the historic faith of the Church, he enquires whether his key-concept succeeds in maintaining the three vital dogmas which Chalcedon was concerned to maintain, namely the Unity of God, the Divinity of Christ and the Unity of his Person.

He is clearly right in claiming that by asserting an 'economic Trinity' and refusing to go beyond the known to the unknown we do not imperil the Unity of God. I have, however, suggested reasons for thinking that, in the way in which he does this, Mr. Montefiore finds it at least very difficult to affirm unambiguously either God's existence or his transcendence.

As regards the Divinity of Christ, Mr. Montefiore points out that he has carefully avoided phrases like 'divine nature' and 'of one substance with the Father,' but he asserts that, in saying that in Jesus the divine activity was fully present so far as is possible in human personality, he was simply translating the essence of Chalcedon into a different thought-form. I find this very difficult to accept. For, while his formulation is certainly consistent with that of Chalcedon, it is equally consistent with a view which Chalcedon, by its formula of the two natures which concur into one Person, deliberately excluded, namely the 'Nestorian' view (whether Nestorius held it or not is immaterial) that Jesus was a man who was kept by grace in a perfect moral union with the eternal Word. A man might gladly assert that in Jesus the divine activity was fully present *so far as is possible* in a human personality if he held that a literal incarnation of God in human nature was metaphysically impossible. The word 'present' seems in any case to be somewhat strange in this context, for it would seem to go more happily with the rejected concept of substance. It would, I should have thought, be more in accordance with Mr. Montefiore's programme to describe an 'activity' as 'operative' rather than as 'present.' I think we have evidence here for my earlier criticism, that his chosen category, however contemporary it may be, lacks the precision of the categories of Chalcedon.

I find the same ambiguity in his attempt to justify his formula as safeguarding the unity of Christ's person. He refers with approval to D. M. Baillie's use of the analogy of grace to illustrate the union of the divine and human in Jesus and Dr. Pittenger's use of the even wider analogy of the whole range of divine-human relations experienced and known, and holds that these are specially congenial to his view that the love and activity of Jesus were the love and activity of God. The trouble with these analogies is that they are far too wide; the former would apply equally well if Jesus was just a very holy saint, and the latter if he were any kind of human being at all. Mr. Montefiore likes these analogies because grace is first of all a paradox and is secondly an activity of God and not an ontological reality, but however applicable they may be to his key-concept they do nothing to show whether or not it preserves the Unity of Christ. If I were discussing Mr. Montefiore's views about grace, I should want to enquire why the activity of God cannot also be an ontological reality and to refer to some very interesting work by modern Roman Catholic scholars on the notion of an *ens dynamicum*. I should also comment upon his strange identification of an 'ontological reality' with a 'bare intellectual concept,' which seems to involve among other things a confusion of the *ordo essendi* with the *ordo cognoscendi*. This would, however, take me too far from our immediate concern.

In concluding his essay Mr. Montefiore repeats that his intention was not to 'go beyond' the conclusion of Chalcedon, but to 'translate' it into a language more comprehensible to-day, the language of dynamic activity in place of the language of substance. The intention was thoroughly laud-

able and I wish I could think it was successful. But it seems
a matter of opinion—I doubt very much whether the ordinary
to me to fail in two respects. First—though this is perforce
intelligent modern man will in fact find Mr. Montefiore's key-
concept of 'moving pattern of activity' more congenial and
comprehensible than the traditional concepts of Christian
theology. Secondly, and perhaps more importantly, his conceptual scheme is far less flexible and far less precise than
that of Chalcedon and is unable to make some important distinctions which Chalcedon on the whole succeeds in making.
This latter defect is, I think, shared by a good many modern
attempts at 'restatement.' Dr. W. N. Pittenger's book *The
Word Incarnate*, for instance, leaves the reader time after
time baffled as to whether Dr. Pittenger is trying to commend
Chalcedonian Christology or Nestorianism or is simply failing to see the difference between them. And Mr. A. C. Bridge,
in his very stimulating book *Images of God*, in his attempt to
reinterpret Christology by analogies from works of art, seems
unable to decide, or at any rate to say, whether the transcendent reality of which, as he tells us, the manhood of Jesus is
the image is God the Father or the eternal Logos.[2] To return
to Mr. Montefiore, I am far from holding that the language of
Chalcedon is incapable of improvement or that the adoption
of the Chalcedonian formula, necessary as I believe it to have
been, was unattended by certain definite drawbacks. It does,
however, succeed in making the necessary distinctions and
stating the essential facts, and this, as I see it, Mr. Montefiore's 'translation' fails to do. If, as is probably the case, the
notions of substance and nature, as they were conceived at
Chalcedon, are too static and impersonal to be fully adequate,
the remedy would seem to be, not to throw over those notions
altogether but to develop and enrich them in a more dynamic
and personal way. There would then be fresh gains without
the loss of anything already achieved. Mr. Montefiore's idea
that a return to Biblical thought-forms will make Christology

[2] Cf. my *Theology and Images*, p. 26.

more intelligible to the modern man, because the Bible thinks in terms of act rather than of being, is ingenious but somewhat dubious, for it involves the abandonment of hard-won intellectual positions and is reactionary rather than progressive. Are the minds of first-century Jews so much closer to those of twentieth-century Europeans than those of fifth-century Greeks? Dom Gregory Dix was correctly quoted by Mr. Montefiore for the view that Jewish Messiahship yields a Christology of *function* in terms of *history* and not of *status* in terms of *origin*. But Dix added that the identification of Jesus's action with God's action (which was what his claim to Messiahship implied) led inevitably, when he was preached as 'Messiah' to Greeks, to identification of his metaphysical status with that of God, and Dix certainly did not regard this development as a misfortune or a mistake. If we believe that the almost violent transplantation of Christianity from a Hebrew to a Greek setting between the middle and the end of the first century took place under the providential dispensation of God, we may be more ready than we should otherwise be to see that it was only in that new setting that the Christian religion could achieve an intellectual formulation at all. Such a study of primitive Hebrew Christianity as is provided by Père Daniélou's *Théologie du Judéo-christianisme* makes it plain that the Jewish mind, for all its many great qualities, was simply not adapted to that task. This does not mean that Chalcedon has the last word. But I do suggest that we need to move on from Chalcedon, rather than back from it; and this is, in fact, what Christian theologians have done. I think it is true that the theologians of the fifth century, with their strongly Platonic background, conceived being in too static a sense; but the remedy for this is not to abandon the notion of being but to interpret it more dynamically. And, just as St. Augustine, in his treatise on the Trinity, brought new life to the Aristotelian category of relation by interpreting it substantially and not accidentally, so it is arguable, following M. Gilson, that St. Thomas revivified the transcendental of Being by understanding it not just as conceptual essence but as existential act. And, if, as was probably the case, St. Thomas never saw the full range and implications of his great new intuition, there is a task for us to-day. Thus, the cure for a static notion of God is not to be found in restricting our speech about him to his activity within the created order, even that activity as shown in the life of Christ; it is to understand God's being itself in terms of act. And this, I believe, is what the Old Testament does.

Thus we can very well accept 'the pattern of divine activity' as our key-concept, but so far from it following, as Mr. Montefiore thinks it does, that 'we shall not speak about the being and nature of God himself,' the precise opposite will be the case. We shall speak about the being and nature of God himself as a pattern of divine activity; this procedure is in fact implicit, and more than implicit, in the classical discussions of the processions in the Eternal Trinity. We shall then be able to take our knowledge of God's activity in Christ, not as a substitute for a knowledge of God himself, but as a means by which God himself is known. 'He that hath seen me hath seen the Father.' We shall see the activity of God in the world as following from his being and shall at the same time see his being as the supreme activity; we shall affirm that *operari sequitur esse* and at the same time recognize that in God *esse* is *actus purus*. And in doing this we may see more significance than Western theologians have always recognized in the teaching of the later Greek theologians about the distinction between the 'essence' and the 'energies' (*ousia* and *energeiai*) in God.[3] And, in so doing, we shall, I believe, be able to escape from the peculiar mixture of agnosticism and immanentism which Mr. Montefiore offers us as a 'translation' of the Christology of Chalcedon.

I shall now pass on to Dr. Lampe's essay, which is entitled

[3] Cf. my remarks about St. Gregory Palamas in *Theology*, LXIII (1963), p. 30f.

'The Atonement: Law and Love.' This runs very much along the line of some of the ideas which he had previously set forward in his Maurice Lectures for 1955, published under the title *Reconciliation in Christ;* they do not, I think, add a great deal to what was said there, and it is difficult to see that they raise any very important questions which theologians ought to be facing but are not facing with the necessary seriousness and determination. Dr. Lampe's starting point is one with which it is difficult to suppose that any Christian theologian would disagree, namely that God is love and that his love is supremely manifested in the death and resurrection of Christ for the reconciliation of men to God. I think it is important to stress the word 'manifested' here, for it might well be argued that the supreme *instance* of God's love is provided by the eternal processions of the Second and Third Persons of the Holy Trinity. Dr. Lampe gives a moving exposition of the way in which the New Testament writers see the reconciliation of man to God by Christ as fulfilling all the great types and intuitions of the Old Testament: the covenant, sacrifice, the Adam made in God's image, estranged by sin and restored in Christ. But these images, whether severally or collectively, are no more than partial gropings after the truth of reconciliation, for they belong to a realm of religious belief which has been radically transformed. It was St. Paul's great achievement to see the true nature of this transformation, and to see that the principle of law has been replaced by that of spontaneous and undeserved love, entirely unrelated to questions of merit or demerit. So Dr. Lampe denounces all forms of legalism and all legal concepts and metaphors in his account of man's justification. He vigorously repudiates the language of the Second of the Thirty-nine Articles, with its assertion that Christ died 'to reconcile his Father to us,' as suggesting that God was estranged from man rather than man from God. He is not, of course, the first writer to comment on this point. E. J. Bicknell, for example, in his classic work on the Articles, takes it very seriously, but stresses the analogical

F

nature of all such language and maintains that God's 'wrath' is not a burst of feeling but 'is rather one aspect of his abiding love, as it deals with the sin that opposes and wars against that love.' 'The mind of God towards sin is unaltered—it is our mind towards sin that has to be transformed, not his— but the change in ourselves makes possible a new personal relationship.' [4] But for Dr. Lampe, all such notions of wrath, law, satisfaction, debt and the like are, in spite of their long history in the theology of Christendom, to be altogether discarded. They subordinate love to justice and they bring back into the gospel the ideas of merit and reward. Now in his book *Reconciliation in Christ* Dr. Lampe has already rejected as theologically unacceptable not only the notion of merit (Christ's merit, no less than man's!) but also the doctrine of justification by imputation, in a way that is somewhat surprising in someone who is recognized as one of the leading Evangelical theologians in the Church of England. Christ, he there tells us, 'does not merely deputise, as it were, for mankind by acting as their substitute. He is a representative in whom, as in Adam, all men are potentially summed up,' though the Evangelical position is safeguarded by the reminder that 'their incorporation into him as the new Adam is by a personal relationship of grace and faith, not by nature.' [5] Now, as I have remarked elsewhere,[6] it is indeed surprising to find Dr. Lampe rejecting as a medieval survival one of the central positions of Reformation theology, but he is emphatic that, in spite of other ideas which are to be found particularly in Luther, 'the Reformers' interpretation of the Atonement was too largely formulated in terms of the reconciling of a wrathful God to guilty sinners,' and he adds that 'this was emphasized, in a manner which contrasts with the teaching of Anselm, by the stress which they laid on the concept of vicarious punishment.' (Not, however, that he would exempt Anselm from the accusation of legalism.)

4 *The Thirty-nine Articles*, 1st ed., pp. 115–16.
5 *Reconciliation in Christ*, p. 53.
6 *The Recovery of Unity*, p. 30.

In accordance with his principle of love and not law, Dr. Lampe insists that 'it is certain that we ought not to ascribe purely retributive justice to God.' (Has any one, I wonder, with the exception of a few violent Protestant substitutionists, ever ascribed to God a *purely* retributive justice?) 'Sin is not mere transgression of the law.' (But, with the same exception, has any one ever said that it was *mere* transgression? I suspect that there is a somewhat question-begging character about these epithets 'purely' and 'mere,' and a tendency to drop them quietly after the reader has been persuaded to assent to the sentences in which they were contained.) Sin 'is a personal condition of estrangement brought about by a man's desire for self-justification.' I have no difficulty in accepting this as a synthetic proposition, but it appears to be offered as a definition, and as such it seems to me to fall under the condemnation of circularity; for 'self-justification' presumably must be taken as meaning something like 'the removal by one's own act of the guilt of one's sin,' and so sin is being defined in terms of itself. In any case, I cannot think that the profound deliberations of generations of Christian saints and thinkers are to be written off quite as easily as this. It is, I suggest, a real weakness of Dr. Lampe's account that he has entirely neglected to consider the necessarily analogical nature of all concepts and images that are applied from ordinary human experience to the mysteries of the Christian religion, even those which he himself favours, and that he has therefore been led to reject as unacceptable a great deal of the classical theology of Christendom and set in the place of its rich complexity an over-simplified and impoverished account of his own. And to revert to the question of merit, is it really as unscriptural as he suggests? 'Be thou faithful unto death and I will give thee a crown of life.' 'Well done, good and faithful servant, enter thou into the joy of thy Lord.' No doubt behind such texts as these there lies the whole mystery of the relation between the grace of God and the free will of man, but, unless we are to face that question more seriously than it was faced by the nominalist theology of the late middle ages and the Reformers, I do not see that we can possibly achieve a theology of redemption which will avoid on the one side the Scylla of Pelagianism and on the other the Charybdis of predestinationism. Hence we find in Dr. Lampe a combination of onesidedness and exaggeration which is quite distressing. Thus, having quite correctly written that 'apart from its grace-faith relationship to God in Christ, the Church has no such qualities [as unity, holiness, catholicity and apostolicity],' he quite inconsequently continues 'It possesses no inherent virtues, for it is a company of sinners dominated by the principle of man's revolt against the Creator.' Again, having rightly told us that the Church's 'holiness is Christ's holiness in which the Church is clothed by grace,' he then adds that 'if it asserts a holiness of its own apart from Christ . . . its holiness becomes no more than a parody of a human virtue,' [7] without any mention of the possibility that Christ's holiness may not only clothe the Church but transfuse it and transform it, so that it becomes radiant with the beauty and splendour of the Lord who has redeemed it and chosen it for his bride. It is indeed important —and ecclesiastics have at times been far less ready than they should have been to admit it—that the Church has been blackened and disgraced by the sins of its members, but Dr. Lampe writes as if the production of real holiness by grace in Christ's members is impossible and as if the great saints of Christendom had never existed. Unless we are prepared to admit that grace, while it is entirely the gift of God, can at the same time produce a real transformation of the Christian, so that the acts by which he glorifies God are at the same time both wholly the work of God as primary cause and wholly the work of the Christian as secondary and dependent cause, we shall find ourselves imprisoned in an artificial and inhuman scheme in which a man's acts, however good and unselfish and God-directed they may be, are of no religious

[7] *Reconciliation in Christ*, p. 70.

value and in which God has neither appreciation nor gratitude to offer in return for the devotion of his children. I cannot think that this is Dr. Lampe's intention, but it seems to be the inevitable outcome of the position which he adopts both in his article and in his book in relation to the whole concept of merit, in spite of the many penetrating and illuminating things which he has to say about other aspects of his subject. And, as I have suggested, it seems to me that this deficiency arises from the neglect, both by Dr. Lampe and his fellow-Leadsmen, to consider with the necessary seriousness and determination two questions of great importance which theologians to-day are called upon to face, namely the analogical nature of all theological concepts and the relation between the grace of God and the free will of man. Had this consideration been given, Dr. Lampe would have been able, without any retractation of his positive affirmations, to include in a coherent synthesis, those other aspects of reconciliation and sanctification which he has so ruthlessly rejected and to achieve a view of both the Christian and the Church which, without any complacency or any trace of Pelagianism, would have been in the true Christian sense of the word, thoroughly optimistic. Such a task has been admirably performed, in a way that is both popular in its presentation and thoroughly theological in its content, by Dr. J. W. C. Wand in a small book which has recently been published under the simple title of *The Atonement*, but whose very modesty may lead it to attract less attention than it deserves.

# CHAPTER V

# UNDERGIRDING THE SHIP

I INTEND in this concluding chapter to discuss comparatively briefly the four essays in *Soundings* to which I have so far paid no attention. My excuse for treating them in this way is that, partly because I feel very much less competent in their several fields of study and partly because they seem in any case to raise fewer controversial issues, I have much less to offer concerning them in the way of comment and criticism than I had in the case of the other essays. In doing this, I shall of course be taking these four essays out of the order which they occupy in the volume, but I do not think that this will matter very much, since, in spite of the Editor's assurance that the symposium is the outcome of a protracted series of meetings and discussions, there is remarkably little co-ordination between its members. There is, in fact, hardly a single cross-reference throughout the book, and the reader is left with the impression that the various Leadsmen have taken their soundings in complete independence of one another.

Professor Ninian Smart, who is the only layman in the whole of Dr. Vidler's crew, has contributed an exceedingly interesting discussion of the Relation between Christianity and the Other Great Religions. He starts with the very salutary reminder that Christianity is not the only great religion which claims to be based upon revelation, however much Christian theologians in Europe have tended to forget this, and that the choice which faces the present-day man is not simply between Christianity on the one hand and purely natural religion or atheism on the other, but also between the Christian revelation and the revelations (rightly or wrongly so described) of, for example, the religions of Hinduism, Islam or China. What, he therefore asks, are the distinctive features of Christianity?

Christians, Professor Smart reminds us, are accustomed to stress the unique way in which Christianity is rooted in history. However, he points out, the Christian account of the events of Christ's life is not simply dictated by the evidence which we have. The historian's conclusions will depend upon his presuppositions, and these, if he is a Christian, include belief in a personal God and a view about the importance of history; furthermore, the cosmic conclusions which Christians draw (such as, that Christ is God) are not necessarily entailed by the New Testament events, even if these last have been established. And many forms of Eastern religion either reject belief in a personal God or look upon such a belief as secondary and transitional. Theravada Buddhism, for example, 'centres on mysticism, but mysticism without God.' And one important form of Hinduism gives the contemplative intuition of the Absolute priority over experience of a personal, holy Being; that is to say, it gives the mystical type of religious experience priority over the prophetic. However, Professor Smart argues, it is in orthodox theism that the most profound combination of the prophetic or numinous type and the mystical type is to be found, and, while recognizing that an argument for theism based upon this assertion cannot be guaranteed to convert a Theravadin to Christianity, he nevertheless looks upon it as extremely persuasive. 'In the confrontation, then, of the theistic religions with those non-theistic systems which I have described,' he writes, 'the claim of theism to represent the fullest truth initially lies in its capacity to weld together the insights both of the prophet and of the contemplative.' He significantly adds that certain narrow views of Christianity, which neglect the contemplative strand, would, if accepted, destroy this claim; and he notes that even Islam became enriched by the Sufi movement. It is, I think, worth noting that there is implied here a total rejection of that doctrinaire and obstinate repudiation of all forms of mysticism which is characteristic of the Protestantism of writers such as Barth, Brunner and Nygren. And, while wisely hesitating to argue for the truth of Christianity on the ground of an alleged ethical superiority of Christians, Professor Smart goes so far as to claim that theism, with its emphasis upon divine transcendence, leaves room for the independence and reality of the world and thus provides an attitude to the world which stimulates moral action as a part of the religious life.

I must confess to some doubt about this last assertion, for it might well be argued that theism implies not so much the independence of the world as its complete dependence upon God, since God is held to be not merely transcendent to the world but also present to all things as their creator, and I should have thought that the moral attitude, which I would agree is a feature of orthodox theism, arose not so much out of an attitude to the world as out of an attitude to the transcendent and holy God. I wish, however, to defend Professor Smart from one accusation which has been brought against him, namely that of a kind of spiritual snobbishness in proposing, as he does, that one test of a system of revealed truth or doctrine is that it 'should reflect the experience of great men in particular and of all religious men in a general way.' It is, I think, perfectly clear from the context that 'great men' does not mean the sort of characters that Carlyle singled out for his hero-worship, but great religious figures such as St. John of the Cross and Gautama Buddha, whom Professor Smart explicitly mentions; and his point is that an adequate religious system (such as he believes Christianity supremely to be) should be able to make sense not only of the religious experience of its adherents but that of all men to whom it may appear that God has in fact revealed himself.

So much, then, for Professor Smart's defence of the belief in a personal God. The other basic Christian belief, that of the importance of history, he defends, first, on the ground that it is congruent with that view of the world as contingent which follows from belief in a personal creator, secondly because the alternative view, that history is cyclic, is tied up with a doctrine of rebirth which is doubtful on empirical grounds, thirdly because even in Eastern countries the course of recent events has led to a revaluation of the significance of time, and fourthly because evolutionary theory reinforces a sense of direction in history.

Professor Smart now remarks on the fact that, although he is supposed to be discussing Christianity, he has hitherto said nothing about Christ. However, he defends this omission on the grounds that it is futile to confront Buddhists or Hindus with the Gospels before giving them an insight into the Christian presuppositions about God and history. He then goes on, however, to argue that the logic of theism inclines in the direction of an Incarnation. 'It is part of the logic of theism, with its emphasis on the numinous experience of God's majesty, that men should regard themselves as sinful. . . . This leaves men in a predicament. On the one hand, before God men feel responsible for their sins and called upon to expiate them. Yet on the other hand, they know in their heart of hearts that only God can save. How marvellous it would be if the paradox could be resolved through God's becoming man! He could thus both expiate and save.' The similarity of this train of thought to that of St. Anselm's *Cur Deus homo* is obvious, but Professor Smart does not claim for it demonstrative force. 'Whether such an Incarnation has happened in actual fact is a question which must be decided by reference to the historical evidence. . . . But we know how to set about answering these questions.' He concludes by asserting that 'journeying into foreign lands and alien cultures can bring one to a better understanding of one's own faith' and that in consequence we must increasingly ponder the problem of translating Christian theology into the terms of the Asian cultures in a way parallel to that in which St. Augustine and St. Thomas translated it into the terms of the Greek philosophers. Here I believe he is entirely right and I find his essay one of the most illuminating in the book. I would only make two final comments. First, that if we are to accept Professor

Smart's line of thought—and I think that we should—we must quite firmly reject that vociferous type of neo-Protestant revelationism which insists that the sole source of knowledge about God is the preaching of the Gospel and that any alleged experience of God other than that of the Christian who is justified by faith is bogus and pernicious. This is worth stressing in case any one should suppose, in a misty kind of way, that you can blend in one red burial Smart on the one side and Nygren and Kraemer on the other. Secondly, it is a little surprising that Professor Smart makes no reference to any of the work that has already been done in the field into which he invites us to enter. It is unfortunately true that Anglican efforts have been almost non-existent, in spite of the widespread and devoted labours of Anglican missionaries in the realm of practical evangelism; the comparative study of religions, like the study of dogmatic and ascetical theology, has been shockingly neglected by Anglican scholars. There has, however, been magnificent work from the pens of Roman Catholic scholars, such as Massignon, Maréchal, Karrer and Professor R. C. Zaehner, and it is strange that Professor Smart does not mention it. (I cannot blame him for ignoring the recent works of the Methodist scholar Dr. Parrinder, which were presumably not available when he was writing.) It will no doubt come as a surprise to some that the Roman Church, with its notorious intransigeance, should have a far more sympathetic attitude to non-Christian religions than traditional Protestantism has, but it must be remembered that Catholicism holds not only the maxim *Gratia non tollit naturam sed perficit* but also *Facienti quod in se est Deus non denegat gratiam*. In spite of this, Professor Smart's essay is certainly one of the best in the book.

I pass now to the essay on The Meaning and Authority of the New Testament by the late J. N. Sanders, whose early death inflicted a sad blow on Cambridge New Testament critical scholarship. It is an ungrateful task to criticize the work of one whose replies cannot be made available to us, and my comments upon his chapter will be of the briefest. After a summary statement of the attitude of the early Church to Scripture and a mention of the views of the Reformers, Sanders gives a rapid survey of the critical study of the New Testament from the English deists and the Continental rationalists, via the Tübingen school and their successors, to the present day. This leads to a provocative assessment of the present situation which seems to me to be substantially accurate:

> In all the intense theological activity of the last hundred years I do not discern any really new movement, but rather new combinations of the old in an uneasy eclecticism. To-day most Christians, even theologians, acquiesce in either a renovated dogmatism or in a compromise between that and a modified Liberalism. Those who do the latter often seem to think one thing in the privacy of their studies, and to say another in their pulpits. The fashionable biblical theology is no real solution. It does indeed represent an earnest attempt to understand the New Testament in its own terms, but it is unable to communicate its understanding satisfactorily to men who think in terms radically different. It is self-contained and self-consistent, but out of touch with experience.

And Sanders adds that Bultmann's attempt to 'demythologize' the New Testament and to interpret it in terms of existentialist philosophy is only a new example of the old *a priori* approach.

Having thus drastically cleared decks for action, Sanders enquires about the relation between the meaning of any document and the authority which is claimed for it. It is no longer possible, he says, to appeal to some external organ to guarantee the authority of the Bible, whether that organ be the *magisterium* of the Church or the tenets of Evangelical Christianity. The authority must be intrinsic, and some space is devoted to substantiating this assertion as applying even to the utterances of the prophets, who claim to be speaking as the mouthpieces of God, and to Jesus himself. 'Thus prophecy, as exemplified in the teaching of Jesus, claims only an intrinsic authority, which, however compelling to the faithful, is never coercive. . . . It follows then that the authority of the New Testament is intrinsic, and is accepted by faith. Its authority can be recognized only when its meaning is understood, and there is no external power with authority to enforce obedience to it or to dictate a particular interpretation of it.' This might seem to imply that, whatever the human reason might suggest, the eye of faith can accept scripture as infallible, but this is far from Sanders's meaning. Christianity is a religion of freedom and love, and to try to supplement this is faithlessness. But 'what are we left with if we reject both an infallible Church and an infallible Scripture?' The answer is that we have an obligation to examine the credentials even of Scripture and to discriminate between what seems in it to be reliable and what not. The discrepancies which the New Testament contains tend to establish its credibility, since they manifest the remarkable unanimity of the picture which it gives of the faith of the first Christians. I must confess that I find it very difficult to understand this strange association which Sanders makes between criticism and faith. At times he seems to be identifying the activity of faith with that of critical study, at others to be conceiving faith (in spite of his repudiation of Bultmann) as an existential affirmation, totally independent of reason, which enables us to accept the substantial reliability of the New Testament picture of Christ in spite of the destructive activity of the critical intellect. In a sense, he admits, the authority of the New Testament rests upon that of the Church, which formed the Biblical canon, but neither Church nor Scripture is free from error. This, however, does not matter, since 'we have *in Christ himself an infallible authority* [the italics are in the original], and can trust him to use the fallible, mediated authorities of Church, Scripture, and conscience, to keep us from error.' This might seem to mean that, while Church, Scripture and conscience are not infallible, we, if we allow Christ to use them for our instruction, are; but I do not think we are intended to interpret 'keep us from error' absolutely, but only in a relative sense. Even so, the assertion is puzzling, as we have already been told that it is only through the fallible Scriptures that we know anything about Christ's teaching and acts. But this is presumably where faith comes in. 'If we make the choice of faith,' we are told, 'the New Testament will seem to us the Word of God, and infallible in the sense that we are prepared to follow its guidance in matters of faith and morals, though there are some things in the New Testament that belong to faith and morals which its own central or highest testimony corrects.' In both Scripture and the Incarnation the Word became flesh, 'and in both it is perceived only by faith.' And at this point the argument makes a sudden swing round. 'If our decision is against faith, we have still to account for the existence of the New Testament and of the Church which wrote it and lives by it. And in this case the great variety of the alternative explanations offered may give us pause.' So faith apparently rests upon reasons after all, though only probable reasons. And, the argument concludes, even if we reject the Christian interpretation, it is by faith of a kind and not by sight. I think the mention of the Church here points to a unifying principle which Sanders in his exposition seems never quite to have seen. For it is in the Church that we have come to know Christ, and through the Church that we have received the Scriptures, not *vice versa;* this is the ground of the faith which survives even the most destructive manœuvres of critical scholarship. But somehow Sanders never quite managed to say this, and so his argument is left floating in that existential atmosphere which verbally he has already disowned. Or, to revert to the dominant metaphor, the lead never really sinks.

Professor John Burnaby, whom I would never wish to mention without expressing my gratitude and admiration for his superb study of the religion of St. Augustine, *Amor Dei*, writes on the subject of Christian Prayer. He starts from the assertion that, in a broad sense, prayer may be taken as covering any attempt at communion with 'the divine,' even when the divine is conceived as an infinite sea in which the individual can be absorbed and as devoid of any personal character. Such 'mystical' religion, he remarks, has a 'universal' character and does not seem to depend on any particular dogmatic or doctrinal systems, and in consequence Protestant theologians have tended to deny it any legitimate place in Christianity and to maintain that truly Christian prayer must be of what Heiler described as the 'prophetic' type. Professor Burnaby himself certainly does not hold this view, as will be well known to any one who has read the trenchant polemic against Professor John Macmurray and Dr. Nygren which, under the title of 'The Embarrassment of the Anti-Mystic,' forms the Introduction to his *Amor Dei*. It is nevertheless clearly important to enquire what specifically Christian element the distinctive character of Christian faith introduces into the prayer of Christians, and it is to this task that he applies himself in his essay in *Soundings*. And starting from the New Testament he finds the dominant note to be that of petition. In spite of the number of texts which he amasses in support of this starting-point, I cannot but wonder whether he has not been to some extent led astray by concentration upon verbal considerations. 'This [that is, petition],' he writes, 'at least was what the early Church meant by *proseuché*,' but he immediately qualifies this statement by the admission: 'though we can be sure that thanksgiving and praise had their due place in its devotions.' It would therefore seem to be less open to misunderstanding if he had simply said that prayer in the early Church was something much wider than petition, though petition had a very prominent place in it and is what is meant by *proseuché*. And, in view of the way in which the life of the early Church was centred in the Eucharist, it is a pity that Professor Burnaby leaves all mention of the Eucharist to the last paragraph of his essay and appears to treat it as a somewhat exceptional and occasional form of Christian activity, albeit a very necessary and significant one, rather than as the normal and normative prayer of the Body of Christ and of its individual members. In spite of his obvious conviction of its deep importance, he brings it into his discussion too late for it to provide the guiding principle that is needed; it is apical, rather than central, to his account. I cannot help contrasting Dom Gregory Dix's luminous reminder that 'the Eucharist had already been at the heart of the religion of Christians for twenty years before the first of these New Testament documents was written' and his masterly display of the way in which the overtones of the Eucharist permeate the whole of the New Testament material.[1] Not, indeed, that this implies that the early Church was unconscious of the duty of petition; no one has done more than Dix to emphasize the conviction of the Church that there was a duty of intercession for the world which only the Church could perform, 'the notion of the priestly prayer of the whole Church, as the prayer of Christ the world's Mediator through his body, being "that which makes the world to stand."' 'All Christendom was then still at one,' he writes (and he is referring specially to the early fourth century), 'on the way in which the public intercession should be offered—by a corporate act involving the whole Church, in which nevertheless each order—laity, deacon and officiant (bishop or presbyter)—must actively discharge its own separate and distinctive function within the fulfilment of the 'priestly' activity of the whole Body of Christ. It offers to God not only itself in its organic unity, but all the world with its sorrows and its busy God-given natural life and its needs.'[2] But all this great Christian act of petition and intercession is here seen as interwoven with, and centred in, the great Eucharistic act of the Liturgy of Christ's Body,

[1] *The Shape of the Liturgy*, pp. 3–4.
[2] ibid., p. 45.

and it is this that I find missing from Professor Burnaby's discussion, devout and thoughtful though it is.

But, to continue, Professor Burnaby is very much concerned with the difficulties for thought that confront any naïve belief in the effectiveness of prayer, difficulties raised by the consideration of God's omniscient providence as well as by the conceptions of natural law and human freedom, and he points out that the obvious consequence would seem to be that prayer can have no effect except upon the man who is praying and perhaps some telepathic or otherwise 'paranormal' effect upon the psychology of the people for whom he prays. But this, Professor Burnaby rightly insists, will not do, for the Christian is asking *God* to act for the other person's good and 'the heart of all Christian prayer is faith in *God*.' Thus he suggests that our perplexities in prayer arise out of an imperfect understanding of the revelation of God in Christ. 'The Church found God in Christ,' he tells us, 'because it had already found God present in its own life. . . . A man must know something of what it means to have God in himself, before he can confess that he owes that presence to the union of Godhead and manhood in Jesus. To believe in the Gospel of the Incarnation is to believe that God's way of ending the separation between himself and sinful man was not to wait till men should return to him, but to go where they were *and to stay there*.' This is finely written, and devoutly too, but it leaves us in obscurity as to how this experience of having God in oneself is to be linked up with the work and life of the historic figure of Jesus of Nazareth, unless in fact we go on to assert—and Professor Burnaby, so far as I can see does not—that the experience has been enjoyed in the Eucharistic life of the Christian Church, the Body of Christ which is the organic extension of his crucified and risen flesh. The very passage which I have just quoted is immediately described by Professor Burnaby as being 'as "mythical" a manner of speaking as the story of the Virgin Birth,' and, while I could accept that statement as verbally satisfactory, since I do not believe that the Virgin Birth is in fact 'mythical,' this does not appear to be the position of Professor Burnaby. According to him, what the passage quoted is meant to do is 'to express the Church's faith that since the risen Jesus parted from his disciples the following of him in the Christian life is possible only in the measure in which the human spirit is united to the divine.' Now this would appear to involve a complete psychologizing of the doctrine of the Incarnation, but Professor Burnaby hastens to deny that talk about the divinity of Christ is no more than talk about the presence of the Holy Spirit in the Christian and, in words which I cannot help feeling that Mr. Montefiore would have done well to take seriously, he notes that the Church has never been satisfied with the reduction of the Incarnation to the level of a supreme instance of grace. Here he has, I think, slightly wandered from the point, for the question at issue was not whether statements about the deity of Christ were to be interpreted simply as statements about the grace-endowed character of *Christ,* but whether they were to be interpreted simply as statements about the presence of the Holy Spirit in *Christians.* But, to return, Professor Burnaby suggests that the union between human spirit and divine, except in Christ, is insuperably 'asymptotic,' while we can still find in the divine-human person of Christ both the pattern and the source of Christian life in the spirit. I cannot say that I find the mathematical analogy which Professor Burnaby uses fully adequate, if it is meant not just as an account of the human sanctity of Christ but also, as it appears to be meant, as an account of the hypostatic union, for it would seem to be quite compatible with a Nestorian doctrine of the Incarnation, though I do not for one moment suspect Professor Burnaby of being a Nestorian. I am far from holding that the formula of Chalcedon is incapable of improvement, but I do not think that Professor Burnaby, any more than Mr. Montefiore, has managed to improve upon it.

However the subsequent development of Professor Burnaby's

G

argument does not seem to depend upon this particular excursion into Christology. He goes on to argue simply that, as the salvation of the world (or, in his words, 'what we call the salvation of the world') was wrought through the freely willed self-devotion of a man, so God's kingdom must come on earth through the operation of human wills which by the acceptance of the Spirit of Jesus have become one with the will of God. 'Prayer,' he continues, 'will be the means of affirming and confirming this unity—a means whose effectiveness will be in proportion to the sincerity of its utterance.' This, again, is finely said, but it does not seem to me to go far enough. For, although the salvation of the world was wrought *through* the freely willed self-devotion of a man—a man who was also God—it was, as St. Athanasius was never weary of insisting, wrought *by* the eternal Word and Son of God, who, by taking human flesh of a virgin mother, had become *that man*. And, again, although acceptance of the Spirit of Jesus is admittedly the means by which human wills become one with the will of God (and I take it that this 'becoming one' is a oneness of grace and not a oneness of nature), it needs to be made clear that this 'acceptance' is not simply a human mental act but is also and primarily the incorporation by the Holy Spirit of the human being in his totality into the Body of Christ. If we can take this further step, then all that Professor Burnaby goes on to say about Christian prayer will be true, but more will be true besides. For it will now follow that the specific characteristic of *Christian* prayer is not that it is the prayer of human wills which have become one with the will of God, but that it is the prayer of the risen and ascended God-man Jesus Christ being prayed by him in and through his members. And in this there will be no reduction of the Christian to the condition of a mere automaton or instrument, for grace perfects nature and does not destroy it and by his union with Christ his own spontaneity and activity will be not suppressed but liberated and enhanced. I think that in fact Professor Burnaby has got very near to this when he speaks of 'the nature of charity as a birth of the divine in the human' and says that 'wherever a human will suffers itself to be invaded by the will of God, it cannot remain a passive prisoner, but must take service with its divine captor. Or, to use a better metaphor, the life that is released in the soul that has consented to the wooing of God's grace is no longer a life *of* the soul, but the life and power of its union with God.' But he never, as it seems to me, makes a quite clear distinction between the moral and psychological aspect of the Christian life on the one hand and its theological and ontological aspect on the other. Had he done so, he would, I think, have been able to make even more convincing his assertion that contemplation and petition need not be regarded as two essentially different ways of prayer. I would add a final remark about Professor Burnaby's plea for the discarding from Christian worship of forms of prayer that are superficially sub-Christian and especially of much of the Psalter. On the practical level, of course, there may be much to be said for revision and rearrangement of some of the traditional liturgical forms, and it is noticeable that even the Roman Church, now that it is facing the demand for a greater use of the vernacular in worship, appears to be contemplating quite extensive changes in both the form and the matter of public prayer. But I think such a work as Dr. C. S. Lewis's *Reflections on the Psalms* shows that some of the liturgical material which is in the long run most fruitful may appear at first sight to be unpromising and even repellent; and I do not think that any one who has shared in the offices of religious communities, and has reflected on the function that the appeal for the help of God with which they open has exercised in the building up of lives dedicated to God, will reject, as Professor Burnaby does, the *Deus in adjutorium meum intende; Domine, ad adjuvandum me festina* as merely the cry of 'self-conscious "saints" crying to God for vengeance upon their enemies.' However, in the end he comes to the Eucharist as the sacrament whose significance is 'to represent and realize that oneness of life into which the taking of our nature by the Son of God, its bearing through cross and resurrection into the heavenly places, and the coming of the Holy Spirit to be its strength and stay, have brought the Creator and his creatures.' If he had only begun from the Eucharist instead of ending with it, how much more cogent would have appeared the superb formula with which he ends his essay: 'All Christian prayer is the activity of that oneness of Life.'

*Soundings* concludes with an essay by the Editor himself on Religion and the National Church and, as might be expected, he bases his discussion very largely upon the teaching of F. D. Maurice. Maurice, Dr. Vidler reminds us, was accustomed, in a striking and paradoxical mode of speech, to contrast what he described as 'religion' with the Christian Gospel. 'Religions separate men from one another and tempt them to boast of what they possess and other men do not; the Gospel is the proclamation that they already belong together as children of the one God and Father of all, and the Church is the Kingdom or Family in which their unity is to be realized.' Now Maurice was, of course, writing at a time when the alternatives to the Established Church were either an extreme Calvinism which held that Christ died only for a small group of predetermined elect souls, and that the rest of the human race was altogether outside the concern of the Gospel, or else a Catholicism understood in a highly individualistic and almost materialistic way. (How odd must have been the Catholicism with which Maurice was acquainted is clear from the passages in *The Kingdom of Christ* in which he discusses the Roman system, and which could only be characterized as a ridiculous travesty if they were taken as a description of the position held by any Roman Catholic theologian or educated layman to-day.) The consequence is that Maurice placed immense stress upon Christianity as a declaration of what man, even fallen man, is, simply as man, and this is, of course, a very important aspect of it and one that is very prominent in such Christian fathers as St. Irenaeus.

But any one who has tried to grapple with Maurice's thought will, I think, have found himself wondering time after time whether Maurice believed that the Incarnation, the Church and the Sacraments have really made any genuine difference to man's condition or whether he thought that their purpose was simply to make it plain what, in spite of all appearances, man's condition already was and had always been. The puzzle arises from the fact that Maurice sets statements of these two kinds side by side without seeming to be conscious that there is any difference between them. I think the explanation is partly to be found in the fact which I have already mentioned, that he felt bound to repudiate the religious attitude which saw the Incarnation as totally unconcerned with the fate of the vast majority of mankind. But I think also that he never managed to find a theological statement which could adequately express the truth that Christ died not to give men a totally new nature but to renew the nature which they already possessed and to make them become more fully what in essence they already were.[3] The danger of Maurice's attitude at the present day is that it may easily be interpreted in the tempting form which assumes that Christ came to tell us that we are really all right and that therefore there is nothing to worry about, and may therefore encourage a complacency which is every bit as deadening as that against which Maurice was so violently and laudably rebelling.

Dr. Vidler is clearly not of the view that this is in fact a serious danger; what he is very much concerned with is Maurice's insight that religion can itself be made a barrier between man and the living God, and in emphasizing this he is led to associate with Maurice certain modern thinkers whose general theological position is one from which Maurice would surely have recoiled in horror. 'Dr. Karl Barth and Dr. Emil Brunner are theologians who in a different idiom have said in our own time much the same as Maurice about religion as

---

[3] Though in fact the formula 'Be what you already are' can be found in Maurice's writings.

man's most subtle substitute for God's own revelation of himself. Dietrich Bonhoeffer, on the other hand, . . . carried the critique of religion a good deal further.' And an anonymous Anglican missionary is quoted to the effect that Christ can set men free from fear and frustration and self-centredness without the Church as a visible organization and by speaking to them in other terms than those that have become canonized in the Christian tradition. At this point we might expect that Dr. Vidler was about to denounce all forms of religious institutionalism and especially any kind of established church, but the precise opposite is the case. Maurice is now quoted in defence of the institutions of the historic Catholic Church as the true safeguards against legalism, systematism and sectarianism. 'Maurice thought the solution lay not in discarding or making light of ecclesiastical institutions and sacramental ordinances but in interpreting them in a manner that at every point rebuked and corrected the disposition of men to lord it over God's family and God's gifts.' While admitting that the anonymous missionary is much less sanguine about this possibility, Dr. Vidler clearly agrees with Maurice on this point and, while holding that a new ecclesiastical settlement will sooner or later be needed, especially if the Free Churches are to come into the establishment, he considers that, during the foreseeable future, a national church is both workable and desirable and he even praises the much criticized doctrinal and disciplinary vagueness of the Church of England as providing a safeguard against narrowness and legalism.

While no one could accuse Dr. Vidler of conventionality or conformism, I find it difficult to acquit him of a trace of romanticism and wishful thinking. Maurice's view of a national church seems to me to have been still just viable a century or so ago, when almost all Englishmen were convinced, if often unreflective and not very fervent, Christians, and when those of position conformed with some regularity to the worship of the established religious body. It would, on the other hand, have been totally inapplicable to the situation in the first three Christian centuries and I cannot see it becoming workable in this country in the immediate future without such a compromise on both faith and morals as would convict the Church of the grossest opportunism. And in most parts of the world where the Anglican Communion is represented such an arrangement would be manifestly impossible. There are and there have been situations of time and place in which the community as a whole has so largely identified itself, in theory if not always in practice, with some form of Christian profession that the Church can, if it is sufficiently conscious of the dangers of compromise and conformity, work for the regeneration of the national life within the framework of establishment. Spain, Ireland and Greece perhaps provide contemporary examples of this, though the lessons of the past are not entirely encouraging. I do not think that, in the present situation, we should be right in clamouring for disestablishment, though a time might easily come when this would be our clear duty, but I would suggest that our present efforts should be directed to reframing the pattern of the Church's life and worship in accordance with its true theological structure, so that its members may be competent to make their impact upon the political and social order in which they live and work as fervent and intelligent members of Christ's Body, rather than to the devising of a new structure of established religion adapted to a predominantly post-Christian society. But the sad fact is that, neither in Dr. Vidler's essay nor anywhere in the volume which he has edited, is there any discussion whatever of the theological nature of the Church. In consequence the whole discussion rests upon empirical judgments whose validity is, to say the least, disputable. Thus, for example, we are told that the nomination of bishops by the 'civil magistrate' is more likely to result in appointments that will keep the Church open to the nation and directed to its service. Is this the lesson of eighteenth-century England and Wales? Again we are told that a national church, recognized as such by the state, is a standing witness to the fact that a man is not only a political creature, but also a spiritual being who belongs to a realm of eternal values. Is the consciousness of this fact really stronger in England than in the United States, where there is no established church but where the majority of people deliberately support some religious body or other? Again Dr. Vidler tells us that the constitutional conjunction of church and state is a sign that the authority of the state is neither final nor absolute. But does the state in England in fact recognize any such limit to its authority? And are there not states where there is no religious establishment—the United States will again serve as an example—but where such limits are in fact constitutionally recognized? That establishment carried with it both advantages and disadvantages for the Church's performance of its true task is obvious, and it can only be a matter of individual judgment as to which way the balance tips. But to attempt to devise a pattern of establishment that will reflect the religious situation of contemporary Britain with any prospect of permanence seems to me to be pure romanticism and in so far as it succeeded it could only have the result of making the Church of England an even more anomalous member of the Anglican Communion than it is at present. 'There is still,' writes Dr. Vidler, 'in the tolerant, pluralist, democratic kind of society which we now have and want to maintain and strengthen—value and validity in the idea of a national church, recognized as such by the state.' No doubt this is true, but, in a world in which social and political changes are taking place with unprecedented speed and variety, and in which the future is more than ever unpredictable, the Church would surely do better to remind itself that its foundations are upon the holy hills and its stability in the things that are not shaken. And this will need much more consideration of the Church's true nature as the Body of Christ than Dr. Vidler and his crew of Leadsmen have given it.